A Girl Named

Faithful Plum

Other Yearling Books You Will Enjoy

Gifts from the Sea by Natalie Kinsey-Warnock

A Good Horse by Jane Smiley

Harry Sue by Sue Stauffacher

The Other Half of Life by Kim Ablon Whitney

The Penderwicks series by Jeanne Birdsall

The Red Umbrella by Christina Diaz Gonzalez

When You Reach Me by Rebecca Stead

The Wonder of Charlie Anne by Kimberly Newton Fusco

A Girl Named Faithful Plum

The True Story of a Dancer from China and How She Achieved Her Dream

Richard Bernstein

A YEARLING BOOK

This is a work of nonfiction, though some names have been changed—specifically those of Teacher Zhu, Comrade Tsang, and a few minor characters—and conversations have been imagined. Also, events that actually took place over a two-year period have been compressed into the single year covered by this book. But everything else, starting with Zhongmei's departure from her hometown on that fateful day in 1978, is described as it actually happened.

Text copyright © 2011 by Richard Bernstein
Cover photograph copyright © 1995; from the author's private collection

All rights reserved. Published in the United States by Yearling, an imprint of Random House Children's Books, a division of Random House, Inc., New York. Originally published in hardcover in the United States by Alfred A. Knopf, an imprint of Random House Children's Books, New York, in 2011.

Yearling and the jumping horse design are registered trademarks of Random House, Inc.

Visit us on the Web! randomhouse.com/kids

Educators and librarians, for a variety of teaching tools, visit us at randomhouse.com/teachers

The Library of Congress has cataloged the hardcover edition of this work as follows:
Bernstein, Richard.
A girl named Faithful Plum : the true story of a dancer from China and how she achieved her dream / by Richard Bernstein.
p. cm.
ISBN 978-0-375-86960-0 (trade) — ISBN 978-0-375-96960-7 (lib. bdg.) — ISBN 978-0-375-98434-1 (ebook)
1. Li, Zhongmei. 2. Dancers—China—Biography. 3. Dancers—United States—Biography.
I. Title.
GV1785.L485B47 2011
792.802'8092—dc22
[B]
2010048722

ISBN 978-0-375-87158-0 (pbk.)

Printed in the United States of America

First Yearling Edition 2012

Random House Children's Books supports the First Amendment and celebrates the right to read.

To Elias,
a.k.a. Tiandao, a.k.a. Dao Dao

Glossary of Chinese Places, Terms, and Names

Note: When Chinese is transcribed into English, the letter *x* is pronounced as though it were *sh*, so *xiao-jie*, which means "younger sister," is pronounced *she-ow-jee-eh*. The letters *zh* are pronounced like *j*, and *q* sounds like *ch*. So Zhongmei is pronounced *joong-may* and Zhongqin, her older sister, is *joong-chin*.

Baoquanling (pronounced *bow-chyuan-ling*) / Precious Water from the Mountain Peaks—Zhongmei's hometown.

Beijing—China's capital city.

Beijing Dance Academy—China's premier dance-training institute.

bing-gwer—an icicle.

bu-tsuo (pronounced *boo-tswaw*)—not bad, pretty good.

Chairman Mao / Mao Zedong—the leader of China's Communist revolution and the all-powerful head of the government from 1949 until his death in 1976.

Communist Party—the organization led by Chairman Mao that took power in China in 1949 after a long and bloody civil war.

Cultural Revolution—a social movement that led to ten years of turmoil in China, from 1966 to 1976, when the leaders fought among themselves and many schools, including high schools and colleges, were closed.

da-ge (pronounced *dah-guh*)—older brother.

da-jie—older sister.

ding zi bu—basic (first) position in ballet.

er-jie—second sister.

er zi bu—second position in ballet.

fen, yuan—terms for Chinese money. One yuan is worth about fifteen American cents; there are 100 fen per yuan, so seven fen is worth about one American penny.

flying apsara—a Buddhist celestial maiden.

Gang of Four—a group of officials led by Mao's wife, Jiang Qing, who wielded great power during the Cultural Revolution but were arrested and imprisoned after Mao's death.

***guanxi* (pronounced *gwan-she*)**—connections with powerful or influential people.

Hegang (pronounced *huh-gong*)—a town near Baoquanling and the first stop on Zhongmei's journey to Beijing.

Heilongjiang / Black Dragon River—Zhongmei's home province in North China.

Heilong River—the broad, turbulent river that divides Heilongjiang from Russia, which was part of the Soviet Union in 1978 and 1979; also known as the Amur River.

Jiang Qing (pronounced *jee-ang ching*)—Chairman Mao's wife, imprisoned after his death and now deceased.

***kang* (pronounced *kong*)**—a heated brick sleeping platform used in houses in North China.

pi-gu (pronounced *pee-goo*)—slang for one's behind, rear end.

The Red Detachment of Women and **The White-Haired Girl**—ballets favored by Chairman Mao's wife, Jiang Qing, and widely performed in China in the 1960s and '70s.

Red Guards—bands of students who roamed China during the Cultural Revolution and attacked people they accused of opposing Chairman Mao and his policies.

wu zi bu—fifth position in ballet.

xiao-di (pronounced *she-ow-dee*)—younger brother.

xiao-jie (pronounced *she-ow-jee-eh*)—younger sister.

xiao-mei (pronounced *she-ow-may*)—little miss.

The Li Family

A Note on Chinese Names

In China, last names come first. That's why the main character of this book is referred to as Li Zhongmei. Li is her family, or "last," name; Zhongmei is her given, or "first," name. Chinese last names almost always consist of a single Chinese character and a single syllable—some of the most common being Li, Chen, Wong, and Liu. Other last names in this book are Jia, Tsang, Zhou, Peng, and Zhu. Given names are typically two characters and two syllables, as in Zhongmei, but they can also be single characters. Zhongmei's younger brother, Li Feng, is a case of the single-syllable given name.

Chinese children customarily have the same last names as their fathers. When women get married, they rarely change their own last name to match that of their husband. This can be seen in the names of Zhongmei's parents. Her father is Li Zhengping, her mother Gao Xiuying.

Li Zhongmei (pronounced *lee joong-may*)—Zhongmei means "Faithful Plum."

Li Zhengping—Zhongmei's father.

Gao Xiuying (pronounced *gow she-oh-ying*)—Zhongmei's mother.

Li Zhongqin (pronounced *lee joong-chin*) / *Da-jie*—Zhongmei's older sister.

Li Zhongling / *Er-jie*—Zhongmei's second sister.

Li Guoqiang (pronounced *lee gwaw-chee-ong*) / *Da-ge*—Zhongmei's older brother.

Li Feng / *Xiao-di*—Zhongmei's younger brother.

Lao Lao—Zhongmei's grandmother.

Lao Ye—Zhongmei's grandfather, who died before the events in the book took place.

Other Characters

Chen Aiyi (pronounced *chen I-yee*)—Huping's mother, who takes Zhongmei in when she first arrives in Beijing.

Da-ma—Policeman Li's wife.

Huping—the young man who accompanies Zhongmei on her first train trip to Beijing.

Jia Zuoguang (pronounced *jee-ah dzwaw-gong*)—vice director of the Beijing Dance Academy.

Jinhua—a fellow student who torments Zhongmei.

Li Guang—the son of Da-ma and Policeman Li, works in a photography studio.

Li Zhongshan / Policeman Li—Da-ma's husband and the friend of Zhongmei's father, whose home becomes her home in Beijing.

Liu Lingzhang—a dance instructor.

Old Zhou (pronounced *joe*)—the night watchman at the Beijing Dance Academy.

Peng Guimin / Teacher Peng—second-year teacher who mentors Zhongmei.

Tsang Tungzhi / Comrade Tsang / Old Maid Tsang (pronounced *dzong*)—administrator of the Beijing Dance Academy.

Wang Tianyuan—the girl Zhongmei meets on line outside the Dance Academy during the auditions.

Xiaolan (pronounced *she-ow-lon*)—Zhongmei's best friend. Xiaolan means "Little Orchid."

Zhu Huaimin (pronounced *joo hwai-min*) / Teacher Zhu—the teacher of the fundamentals of ballet.

李忠梅

A Note to the Reader

Sometimes the best stories are the ones that are right in front of your nose. For most of my career as a newspaper reporter and writer of books, I've had to travel far, sometimes literally halfway around the world, to find my material. But I didn't have to go anyplace to learn the amazing story of Li Zhongmei. It came to me, and it stayed right in front of my nose, even though for a long time I didn't do anything with it.

I met Zhongmei almost twenty years ago, before many of the readers of this book were born. She was then, and she still is, a sweet and gentle person. But over the years I've known her, she's told me her not so sweet and gentle story, of an ardent girl from a very faraway place whose dream of becoming a dancer turned into the kind of nightmare that, had she not been very brave, would have destroyed her.

I always thought it was a remarkable tale full of amazing incidents and, in the end, a sweet and happy one too. Still, for years I was busy with my job, writing articles for the *New York Times*, where I was a foreign correspondent, and, from time to time, writing books aimed at adult readers. Until, finally, my sister, Judy, told me one day, "I think young readers, kids around Zhongmei's age when she first went to the Beijing Dance Academy, would find her story fascinating. Why don't you do a book on her?"

And so I did. The result is in your hands. I hope you like it. Also, I hope it will inspire you never to give up in the face of adversity and unfairness, but to look deep within yourself, as Zhongmei did, and find the strength, the discipline, and the determination to overcome.

Prologue

*D*ear *Big Sister,* wrote Li Zhongmei from Beijing, China's capital.

I miss you. I miss everybody. I even miss Teacher Wong, who was kind of mean sometimes in fourth grade. Sometimes I wish I had never come to Beijing. I feel so far away from home. I don't know why Teacher Zhu hates me so much. What did I ever do to her? She still won't even let me take ballet class, and if I don't take ballet class, how can anyone expect me to pass the exams at the end of the year? The other girls all keep teasing me for being a country bumpkin. And it's true. I am a country bumpkin. When I got here, I didn't even know what getting on television meant. Remember how that made Teacher Zhu mad as a hornet? Well, I told you about that already, didn't I? But there's one thing I didn't tell you.

There's a person here that we call Old Maid

Tsang. She would kill me if she knew I called her that. She did something really terrible, so bad I'm afraid I'll start crying if I tell you in this letter. It's not that I'm ashamed of crying. I cry all the time here, after lights are out and all the other girls are asleep. But I'm afraid of getting the paper all wet. Anyway, I'll tell you about that on my next trip home.

Don't tell Ma and Ba that I'm having a hard time here. I don't want them to worry. Don't tell Lao Lao either. It would make her sad. But don't worry. Do you remember the plan we made when we saw each other for New Year's? I'm sure you do. Well, it's going pretty well. Old Zhou pulls on the string outside my window every morning at four o'clock, the one that's tied to my wrist, so I always wake up on time. It makes me pretty tired. The other girls get two hours more sleep than I do. But I'm strong, and I have to do it. I'll do anything not to get thrown out of here.

I'll see you at home this summer. I'll have a lot more to tell you, especially about Old Maid (I mean Comrade) Tsang. Please make my favorite noodles in chicken soup, if there's any chicken. If not, I'll be happy to have just plain noodles in soup without chicken, but I'm hoping for chicken too. Greedy me.

Your little sister

1

Leaving Home

One sunny morning in the spring of 1978 in the remote, very northernmost part of China, a slight eleven-year-old girl named Li Zhongmei got on a bus for the first leg of a journey to Beijing, China's capital. Zhongmei had gotten up that morning as she always did, to the sound of roosters crowing and hens clucking in nearby yards. She was so excited, hopeful, and nervous that she could barely eat the breakfast of rice porridge and corn fritters that her older sister Zhongqin made for her, because this was indeed a very big event in the life of a young girl who had never been more than a few hours from her hometown. It was even a noteworthy event for the town itself, a place called Baoquanling, most of whose residents had never been to Beijing and never expected to go.

When Zhongmei got to the bus station, just a patch of open ground alongside the town's main street, she found that most of the people she knew were there to see her off—her classmates from the fourth grade in elementary school, her neighbors, and a few of her teachers. Her two older sisters, her older brother, and her younger one had accompanied her to the bus station as well, though her mother and father couldn't be there because, like all the adults in this region of China, they had to put in a full day of work, whether their daughters were heading off to Beijing or not. In all, the trip would take three days and two nights on two buses and two trains. But Zhongmei wouldn't be alone. On the first part of the journey to Jiamusi, which was two buses and four hours away, she was going to be accompanied by Zhongqin, who was not only the older of her sisters but was also her best friend.

"We're going to miss you," one of her classmates called out as Zhongmei and Zhongqin turned to get on the bus.

"I'll miss you too," Zhongmei replied.

"Do your best," one of her teachers said, raising a clenched fist in the air, looking a bit like a figure in one of the posters that were up all over China in those days, urging people to fight for the revolution. "Try hard. Be strong."

"I will," said Zhongmei.

Zhongmei shook hands all around, gave her younger brother a pat on the head, hugged her second sister, and smiled at her older brother, who gave her a cheerful thumbs-up. Standing on the first step of the bus entrance, she took one last look around the place where she had spent her whole life. Baoquanling was about as remote as remote gets in China, pressed against the border with Russian Siberia in China's Heilongjiang Province, blazing hot in summer, freezing in winter, battered by strong winds in the spring and fall. The air on this early morning was cool and fresh. The sky was a pale blue stained with yellow dust and streaked with high, thin clouds. A Chinese flag, five white stars on a field of red, hung limply from a nearby flagpole. Through a gap in the buildings that lined Baoquanling's main street, Zhongmei could see a row of men and women, pitchforks and rakes slung over their shoulders like rifles, marching out to the wheat and vegetable fields of the Baoquanling State Farm.

Zhongmei and Zhongqin pushed their way into the bus, Zhongmei carrying the small cloth suitcase that Zhongqin had bought for the occasion at the local department store—none of the Li children had really been anyplace before, so they didn't have any travel accessories. There was a good deal of pushing and shoving as passengers scrambled to find seats, or risk having to stand in the aisle all the way to Hegang. Zhongqin was lucky to get a spot in the very first row just behind the driver. She relieved Zhongmei of the suitcase and put it on her lap. Zhongmei, a bit less lucky, sat on the cushioned engine cover that occupied the front part of the aisle, which warmed up from the heat of the engine and vibrated the whole way to Hegang.

Zhongmei watched as the bus driver revved up the engine and put it noisily into gear. She turned to wave to her friends and family, but the bus kicked up such a thick cloud of dust and smoke as it roared into motion that nobody was visible. Zhongmei felt a wave of disappointment at that, but then she figured it didn't really matter. For weeks everybody had been telling her that she was bound to fail in Beijing and would be back in Baoquanling pretty soon, after which everything else would go back to the way it had been before—except that her hard-pressed family would have to pay back the money they borrowed for one expensive train tricket. This was not what Zhongmei hoped for, and she was determined not to fail. And yet so many people seemed to think that she was making this big trip for nothing that she had begun to wonder if, maybe, they were right.

The flat, straight road leading out of Baoquanling was lined with gray birch trees whose trunks were painted white so they could be easily seen at night. It teemed with bicycles, oxcarts, and three-wheeled farm trucks filled with trussed pigs, slatted chicken crates, bricks, cinder blocks, mounds of cabbages or turnips or eggplants or straw, or mesh bags filled with scallions or spring pea shoots or bulging with garlic heads. Blackbirds perched on the electricity wires strung across the endless rank of telephone poles parallel to the road.

The bus rumbled and bounced on the rutted track. Trucks, crowded with farm workers whose legs dangled over the edges of their flat wooden beds, passed from the other direction. They were being taken to Baoquanling's more distant fields, and Zhongmei strained to see if her mother was among them, since she was a fieldworker herself who often traveled that way, but she caught no glimpse of her. Her bones beat to the vibration of the engine. Her bottom was warm.

In the distance on the left side of the bus was a range of purple hills where, in the spring and summer, members of Zhongmei's family searched for medicinal herbs and mushrooms. These were the peaks in the name of Zhongmei's hometown, whose three Chinese characters, *Bao Quan Ling*, mean "Precious Water from the Mountain Peaks," and Zhong-mei remembered her excursions there with her two sisters. As the youngest, Zhongmei was only allowed to go to the crest of the first hill, where the sisters gathered pine nuts and mush-rooms. Wolves lived beyond that spot and over the next hills, and often at night the Li family could hear their distant howl-ing. Sometimes one of Zhongmei's older cousins went deep into the mountains to hunt for wild turkey and pheasant, and when he was successful, there was meat for dinner, a rare event for the people of Baoquanling.

Once Zhongmei's younger brother, Li Feng, got sick, and her second sister, Zhongling, took it upon herself to go into the mountains to gather a special grass that could be brewed into a medicinal tea. Zhongling climbed through the woods and over the first hill, where the sisters usually stopped for their mushrooms and nuts. She walked over the second hill and into a valley where, as she gathered the grass, she noticed two pup-pies in a nest of leaves and twigs under a big tree. Or at least she thought they were puppies. They were cute and playful. Happily Zhongling put them into her sack and brought them home, shepherding them under a table in the kitchen and feeding them some scraps.

That night, the howling of the wolves wasn't as far away as it usually was. It was alarmingly close. There was a scrap-ing noise just outside the house, canine nails sliding down the brick walls. Suddenly the gray head of a wolf, its fangs showing, appeared in a window, just like Zhongmei imagined

7

in the story of the three pigs, which she'd read at school. It seemed to be looking inside the house, trying to find what everybody now knew were wolf pups, not dog pups. Zhongmei remembered not sleeping much that night as she huddled against her big sisters, listening to the wolves as they prowled outside, sniffing at the window, scratching the walls, howling at the moon just outside the gate.

"Don't be scared," Zhongqin said to Zhongmei and to Li Feng, who was equally terrified. "It's a strong brick house."

Zhongmei finally fell asleep, and when she woke up at dawn, the wolves had left. A car belonging to the state farm was called. Zhongling put the two adorable wolf pups in her sack, scurried through the yard, ran out the gate, and jumped into the car, looking out for the wolves she feared might still be roaming the alley outside the house. Carrying the sack over her shoulder, she climbed over the first hill and, not daring to go any farther, released the two pups, and then watched as they scampered over the hill toward the deep forest. That night, Zhongmei remembered, now smiling at the thought, the howling of the wolves was reassuringly far away, though it was still a little scary.

On the right, Zhongmei caught glimpses of the sun glinting on the Heilong River, which formed the border between China and Russia. Between the hills and the river were the vast flat farm fields of the state farm, the cement factory, brick kiln, elementary school, and low-slung residential areas that made up the only world Zhongmei had ever known.

Zhongmei had never been so full of nervous anticipation

as she was now, facing both thrilling possibilities and scary unknowns. She had never been on a train before, or, for that matter, even seen one close up, and now here she was, soon to be on one that would take her all the way to China's fabled capital, which, to a country girl like her, seemed unimaginably glamorous. Beijing was where China's most famous people lived. It was the home of the country's greatest palaces and monuments, not to mention gigantic Tiananmen Square, which Zhongmei had seen in countless pictures in the newspaper. Movie stars lived in Beijing and so did China's leaders, including of course Chairman Mao, the founder of the People's Republic of China, whose picture was everywhere, though he had died two years before, and whose most famous pronouncements were memorized by every Chinese schoolchild. It was big and important, but it was also a place where Zhongmei didn't know a single person, which was not comforting for an eleven-year-old girl who had never been alone. But even in her state of excitement, Zhongmei could not have known that everything in her life was going to change from this moment of departure. If she had any idea just how hard these changes were going to be, she might never have gotten on that bus to Hegang in the first place.

李忠梅

2

An Impossible Dream

A few weeks before, Zhongmei had been sitting at home early in the evening copying Chinese characters into her school notebook when Zhongqin, who was nine years older than Zhongmei and the person who most took care of her, casually mentioned seeing an interesting notice in the *People's Daily* newspaper, which she'd read at work.

"It said that the Beijing Dance Academy is going to have open auditions," Zhongqin said. She was standing in front of a large pot in which she was boiling dumplings for dinner.

Zhongmei immediately perked up. She loved to dance. She danced at her elementary school's performances. She went to ballet classes in the Workers and Peasants Cultural Center, given by a woman who had been sent to Baoquanling from one of China's big cities. She danced in the lane outside her house, just for fun, humming to give herself some musical accompaniment.

"Open auditions? What's that?" she asked.

"The school was closed during the Cultural Revolution," Zhongqin said. The Cultural Revolution was ten terrible, violent years in China from 1966 to 1976 when the country's top leaders struggled against each other for power and the whole of society was turned upside down. Bands of eager teenagers called Red Guards roamed the country ganging up on anybody, including their teachers and even their parents, if they felt they didn't give their total, loving support to Chairman Mao. They destroyed old things like antiques, temples, and priceless works of art because they felt that there should be nothing old in the brand-new China being built under Chairman Mao's brilliant supervision. The universities and schools like the Beijing Dance Academy, and even the elementary and high schools, closed for three years.

"Even after it opened again a couple of years ago, the students were chosen directly by the school," Zhongqin said. "But now anybody who wants to go can audition."

Zhongqin began to ladle dumplings into blue earthenware bowls and passed them to her four brothers and sisters. Zhongmei put down her notebook. She plucked a pair of chopsticks out of the clay vase on the counter where they were kept, and picked up a dumpling.

"Anybody can go?" she asked, holding the dumpling in midair and looking at it as though it were a rare specimen of butterfly. She dipped it in some soy sauce spiced with chopped chili peppers and devoured it.

"It's only for eleven-year-old boys and girls," Zhongqin informed her.

11

"Well, I'm eleven years old!" Zhongmei shouted. "I want to go!"

"She wants to go," Zhongqin said to the other children dismissively.

"Well, why not?" Zhongmei said.

Zhongqin thought for a moment.

"Why not? The paper says that something like sixty thousand girls are going to go to the auditions all over the country, in Beijing, Shanghai, Guangzhou, Nanjing, and Chengdu"—China's biggest cities. "And out of those sixty thousand girls they're going to select a grand total of twelve. Twelve! Maybe two or three from each audition. So how good do you think your chances will be?"

"Well, somebody's going to get it," Zhongmei said. "My chances are the same as everybody else's."

"No, they're not," Zhongqin replied. "You're a little nobody from a nothing little town like Baoquanling. You really think you're going to be one of those twelve girls?"

"If everybody thought that way, nobody would go," Zhongmei said.

"Yes, they would," Zhongqin replied, "because they live in big cities and don't have to travel for days to get to the audition, and they attend famous ballet schools, where they know the people who can help them get into a place like the Beijing Dance Academy. People like us from so far away don't know anybody. And anyway, you have school. You'd miss two weeks."

"Well," Zhongmei hesitated, not knowing what to say about school, where she had always been a dutiful student.

"But I go to ballet school too," she continued, avoiding the issue by changing the subject. "And I'm the best in my class."

"The best according to you," Zhongmei's older brother, whose name was Guoqiang, put in.

"No, not according to me," Zhongmei replied, "according to everybody who knows anything, which you don't."

"Even if it's true, which it probably isn't, being the best in Baoquanling doesn't make you good enough to go to the best dance school in all of China," Guoqiang said.

It was true that Zhongmei was the best dancer in her ballet class, and she had other qualifications besides. For a couple of years she'd been a well-known performer in Baoquanling. She had been chosen at her school to be the girl singer at a noontime performance that was held every day to entertain the town's farmers when they broke for lunch, these farmers working in the far-flung wheat fields, pigpens, and chicken coops that surrounded the town. For a while Zhongmei had gone every day to the microphone in the town hall, a two-story brick-and-mortar edifice adorned by orange stucco pillars and a portrait of Mao. There, in her flutey voice, she sang a song that was carried on loudspeakers set up in every corner of the district—often, but not always, songs in praise, you guessed it, of Chairman Mao. Zhongmei didn't really think all that much about Chairman Mao, though she certainly heard people speaking of him with reverence as China's great helmsman, the man who had led the country's Communist revolution. His picture hung on the wall behind her teacher's desk in her classroom at school. An identical picture was on a wall at home, and it scared her because the chairman's eyes seemed to follow her wherever she went. She sang the words because they were the words to the song:

> He was our good chairman,
> He saved our country and our people,
> He's our own red sun.

After a while, Zhongmei recorded some songs, accompanying herself on the *yang-qin*, which is a kind of Chinese xylophone. Some of her classmates played the *er-hu*, a two-stringed Chinese violin with a horsehair bow and a sound box made of snakeskin, in the background. From then on, the farmers were treated to Zhongmei's recordings, and she didn't have to go to the microphone herself every day. She was famous. She used to be stopped by total strangers on the street wanting to say hello to her. Once her ballet teacher took her to Jiamusi to study for a few days with a song and dance troupe there. It was the only other time in her life that Zhongmei was away from home.

Like good Chinese girls, Zhongmei was properly modest and well behaved, but she was also ambitious. She was convinced that she was meant to do something special in her life, something more thrilling than being a Baoquanling farm girl. Not that there was anything wrong with farm girls. So far that's what she had been, and that's what her two sisters were also. But Zhongmei had always had the idea that she was destined for something else, and the little bit of fame she enjoyed in

Baoquanling encouraged her in this thought. The truth is that she was rather special, pretty in her wiry, tomboyish way and naturally graceful. She was tall for her age and very slender, with long, skinny limbs, her hair, tied up in the pigtails that all girls her age wore in those days, swinging behind her shoulders.

At dinner that night she wore her usual blue cotton pants, made by her mother, a simple white schoolgirl's blouse also homemade, and, around her neck, the knotted red scarf of the Young Pioneers, a sort of Chinese Boy and Girl Scouts that all children Zhongmei's age belonged to. She had a delicate oval face, full lips, and a clear complexion, though her skin, darkened by the sun and dried by the stinging winds of her hometown, marked her as a girl from the countryside. She was a sweet girl, polite, well liked by her friends and teachers, but she wasn't meek or shy. She could run faster than most boys her age. Her dark eyes always glinted with something untamed and fiery, but never more so than on that night when Zhongqin told her about the Beijing Dance Academy auditions.

"Well, I want to go," she said, turning to Guoqiang, "and you can't stop me."

"Forget it," Zhongqin said. She spoke sharply, but then she looked at her little sister and she felt a surge of tenderness. Zhongmei, having snapped at Guoqiang, stared at the swirl of steam rising from her bowl, no doubt conjuring up fantastic possibilities. Nobody could understand her dreams better than Zhongqin, because Zhongqin herself had been a performer and she had also had dreams. In high school she was chosen to play the heroine in the plays and ballets that were very popular at

15

the time. Zhongqin had gotten the most important part in *The White-Haired Girl*, which was a famous story about poor farmers fighting against injustice and mistreatment. Zhongqin's character, named Xi-er, is cruelly treated by an evil landlord and his equally evil mother, who pours hot soup over her face and locks her in a dungeon in her son's fancy house. Xi-er's suffering makes her hair turn white—which it remains even after she is saved by the brave soldiers of the revolution.

The performance was at Baoquanling's Workers and Peasants Cultural Center, near the main intersection of town. The audience had applauded warmly when Zhongqin took her bows, and ever since she had yearned to be onstage again, to dance and sing in front of an audience and soak up its appreciation— but she never had that chance, and one big reason was that she was needed at home to take care of her younger brothers and sisters while her parents put in their long hours on the state farm. She had, quite simply, no time for dance and music lessons or to take part in plays or ballets.

Instead, when she finished high school, Zhongqin went to work for a factory in Baoquanling that made sugar out of locally grown beets and sold it all over China. She was very bright and quick, so she was assigned to the office to keep the factory's files in order. That was how she happened to see the notice about the Beijing Dance Academy auditions in the *People's Daily*. At that time, very few people in Baoquanling read the newspaper. There was no local newspaper and only a few copies of the national papers circulated in offices like Zhongqin's, usually arriving a few days late. In Baoquanling, the news was announced over loudspeakers, or it was written in chalk on large blackboards set up in several places in the town and around the sprawling state farm. Zhongqin saw the notice, and knowing how much Zhongmei loved to dance, she thought she'd mention it.

"I'd like you to be able to go," Zhongqin said now. "Even if you don't make it—and, let's be realistic, you probably wouldn't—you'd have a chance to see Beijing. I'll never have a chance to see Beijing, so it would be nice if you did. You could bring back pictures. But maybe I shouldn't have said anything, because now I've given you all sorts of ideas. But there's no way. I mean, do you think for a second that Ma and Ba can afford to let you go?"

"Well, they have some money, don't they?" Zhongmei said.

"Not very much, and they can't spend it all on you," Zhongqin said. "You see how hard they work, going out before we even wake up and coming home after dark. And for all that work, they can barely afford to feed us. And now there's also Lao Lao and Da Yeh." Lao Lao was Grandma, the Li children's mother's mother, who had come to live in Baoquanling a few months earlier because the Li children's grandpa had died and she was too old to take care of herself. Da Yeh was the children's uncle, who also lived with the Li family at that time, because poor as Baoquanling was, other places were even poorer.

"Well, if I go to Beijing," Zhongmei said, trying genuinely to be helpful, "there will be one less person Ma and Ba will have to feed."

Zhongqin smiled. "Be reasonable, Zhongmei," she said. "It

17

costs a lot to travel to Beijing, and for what? Yes, maybe there'd be a miracle and you'd be chosen, but twelve girls out of sixty thousand? And one of them is going to be a farm girl from Baoquanling? Come on."

For a minute the Li children ate their dumplings in silence.

"But I want to go," Zhongmei said stubbornly. "I mean, why should other girls have a chance like that but not me? It's not fair."

"I understand how you feel," Zhongqin said. "It would be an amazingly wonderful thing to do. But you've got to forget it. It's the silliest idea that ever was."

Silly or not, Zhongmei that night thought only of going to the Beijing Dance Academy. She roamed the Li family's narrow, soot-darkened house and yard, entertaining visions of beautiful costumes and flying jetés and wondering what her parents would say when she asked them if she could go to the audition. The Li family's house was connected to a row of identical houses inside a neighborhood of unpaved lanes shaded by ginkgo and locust trees. There was a brick wall facing the lane, then the small earthen courtyard where Zhongmei's mother had built roosts for her chickens and ducks, along with a pen for the occasional goat or pig.

A small foyer led into the house. It had wooden floorboards that could be lifted up to give access to an underground storage area where the Li family kept a large mound of cabbages in the winter, cabbages and potatoes being the mainstay of the Baoquanling cold-weather diet. When you walked into the house between September and April, the first thing you noticed, after passing the chickens and ducks, was the sour, briny, and sweet odor of slightly fermented cabbage leaves. Zhongmei would never forget it.

A hallway extended from the foyer all the way to the back of the house, where a door led to a fenced-in backyard. There the Li children's tireless mother cultivated green beans, carrots, scallions, pea shoots, eggplants, and other vegetables during the summer. Just after the entryway on the right was a narrow kitchen with a brick floor and a smoky coal-fired stove. A large wok sat on the stove, whose top had been cut out to accommodate the wok's rounded bottom. Next to it was an iron cauldron where water, brought from a well at the end of the lane, was boiled to make it safe to drink. There was no toilet. The homes of Baoquanling did not come with indoor plumbing. There was a public toilet at the opposite end of the lane from the well. It was used by the whole neighborhood and smelled accordingly.

Bathing was done in a large public bath in the center of town, and it wasn't done all that often. The cost was ten Chinese cents per person, five cents for children, which is less than one American penny. Some families went to the public bath just once or twice a year, almost always before the Chinese New Year, which is in the middle of winter and is China's biggest holiday. They brought soap and boxes of baking soda, which served as shampoo, and they luxuriated for hours, using scrubbers of soft wood to scrape away dead skin. When Zhongmei and her younger brother were small, Zhongqin used a basin in the kitchen to wash them, supplementing their sessions in the public baths, though now only the youngest, Li Feng, got help bathing. Bathtubs and showers in the homes were as unheard of as indoor running water.

The rest of the Li family's house consisted of a single long room containing the *kang*. This was a raised brick platform covered with mattresses of stuffed straw. It was heated by coal bricks placed underneath it at night and served as a bed for the entire Li family. Lao Lao and Da Yeh slept on the same *kang*. During the day, the mattresses were rolled up and a low table was put on the *kang*, and that's where the Li family ate their meals and where the children did their homework. It was where Zhongmei was sitting and practicing her calligraphy when her sister told her about the auditions.

Zhongmei's mother and father, whose names were Gao Xiuying and Li Zhengping, worked long hours. Every morning before dawn, while the children still slept, they would be awakened by music blaring over the same loudspeakers that later in the day carried Zhongmei's girlish voice to the farthest corners of the Baoquanling State Farm. Working at the state farm meant that the farmers didn't farm their own land or raise their own animals—except for the few chickens and ducks that they kept in their courtyards. The land and animals belonged to the government, which paid its workers salaries—small ones. It was a bit like being in the army. Groups of men and women, shovels, rakes, and pitchforks over their shoulders, would appear along the paths and lanes of town marching to the fields while military music played on the loudspeakers.

Zhengping, however, had had two years of training as a mechanic, so he was picked up by a truck and rode in the back of it to the transportation brigade, a workshop a few miles away where he repaired cars, trucks, and farm machinery. He rarely got home before dark, except for the two months in summer when it stayed light until ten o'clock.

Zhongmei's mother worked in the fields, and she also left before dawn and came home after dark. She tended to the chickens and ducks and to the vegetable garden in the back, and she made all the clothes worn by all the members of the Li family, including their shoes, their hats, and their mittens. She did a lot of this by hand, especially the shoes, which required big needles to attach the cloth uppers to the thick soles, made of wads of rubber that the children's father salvaged from old tires at the repair shop where he worked. But mostly she pressed into service her most prized possession, a nonelectrical sewing machine that she operated with a foot pedal. She cut out swatches of fabric from larger pieces that she bought at the Baoquanling Department Store and fashioned blouses and trousers, padded jackets, shirts, and pajamas. Zhongmei would never forget the rhythmic sound of the sewing machine's foot pedal rocking back and forth under Xiuying's right foot, and the staccato *tick tick tick* of the needle as she worked. Some years, especially for a few days before the New Year, Xiuying stayed up all night so each of the children would have a new set of clothes. The children would find the new clothes when they got up at daybreak. Their mother, having sewed all night, would already have left for the fields.

Except for five days off during the New Year, there were no holidays at the Baoquanling State Farm, no vacations, not even any long weekends. The only regular day off was Sunday, when Zhengping and Xiuying were busy with chores around the house, so it was only in the evening that they could spend any time at all with their children. Often Zhongmei would go to sleep before both of her parents got home, but on this night she waited up, and when both were home, she stood in front of them, hands at her sides, and asked if she could try out for the Beijing Dance Academy.

"No!" was the immediate and emphatic answer.

3

The Hunger Strike

"Why not?" Zhongmei said, disappointed but not really surprised.

"Because people like us don't do things like that," Zhongmei's father, Zhengping, said.

"Why? What's different about us?" Zhongmei asked.

"To begin with, we don't have money to send you to Beijing," her father replied.

"It can't be that expensive, one little train trip," Zhongmei protested.

"One little train trip! Do you realize how far it is to Beijing?" Xiuying asked. "Your father went there once when he was sent by the state farm, so he knows."

That one time was a big event in the life of the Li family and of Baoquanling. People talked about it for months. A girl from the town had run away there to be with a boy she had fallen in love with. But this was at a time in China when nobody could go to live in a big city without special permission from the government, and when nobody could get married without permission either. So Zhengping, a trusted and respected member of the state farm, had been sent to Beijing to find the girl and bring her back. This took some weeks and required the help of the Beijing police, after which he promised the girl that she could marry the boy if they agreed to stay in Baoquanling.

"It was three days and two nights to get there," Xiuying said, "and the cheapest ticket costs thirty yuan, sixty for a round trip. Your father and I only earn that much money in two months!"

"Secondly, we have no *guanxi*," Zhengping continued. He used the Chinese word that meant "connections," because in China it helped a lot to have powerful friends. "Do you think the Beijing Dance Academy is going to take anybody who shows up?" Zhengping said. "They're going to take the children of their friends, who already live in big cities and don't have to go so far that they'll miss weeks of school, not like you."

"Ba," Zhongmei insisted, "I still want to go."

"Nobody in our family has ever been to Beijing, except for that one time when Ba went," Xiuying said. "Nobody else, not me, none of your grandparents or your uncles or aunts or your brothers and sisters, have ever been to Beijing. They all feel that Baoquanling is good enough for them. But you feel you should go?" Xiuying said.

"It's the chance of a lifetime," Zhongmei said, her voice mixing determination with uncertainty.

"Ma and Ba have more important things than to indulge your fantasy about getting into the Beijing Dance Academy,"

Guoqiang volunteered. Guoqiang was a good student at the local high school, and he liked to use big words like *indulge*.

"You keep out of this," Zhongmei retorted.

"Hey," Guoqiang exclaimed. "Maybe I could go to Beijing too! Hey, Ba, Ma, send me to Beijing! I want to be a movie star!"

"Well, can I go or not?" Zhongmei asked her parents.

"You can't go," they replied in unison, "and that's final."

But now, here was Zhongmei getting on a bus for the first leg of her fateful journey to Beijing, and this was because nobody in the Li family, not her parents, not even Zhongqin, who knew her best, had quite understood how stubborn and determined she could be. From the moment her older sister had first talked about the Beijing Dance Academy, Zhongmei felt that either she would go to the audition or her life would be pointless, without meaning or hope. As the bus roared off in the direction of Hegang, Zhongmei thought about how she had stewed angrily for a few days and then decided to take drastic action to force her parents to yield to her demand. She knew it was a kind of blackmail, and that made her feel a little ashamed, but she did it anyway.

For two days she stayed home, refusing to go to school and refusing to eat. She was so weak at the end of the second day that she could only lie on the *kang* and stare at the stained plaster ceiling of their little brick house. When she sat up, she felt so dizzy she had to lie right back down again. The gnawing in her stomach was almost unbearable. She dreamed of a bowl of the thick noodles in broth that Zhongqin made for the family.

"You won't eat?" her father said to her on the morning of

the third day. It was still dark outside. He was on his way out of the house. "Fine. Starve to death."

"Do you know how hard we work to put food on the table?" Zhongmei's mother said. "Do you see your father and me getting up before dawn and coming home after dark? And you won't eat?"

"No," Zhongmei said. She reminded herself of a radio drama she had once listened to at home, about a farm girl who refused to marry the emperor's son, because she was in love with a simple boy from her village. "I'd rather die," the girl had said, a line that deeply impressed the eleven-year-old Zhongmei.

"Zhongmei, this is silly and bad for your health," her mother told her. "Please eat something."

"You won't have to take care of me anymore," Zhongmei said, that radio drama in her mind, tears wetting her cheeks. "I'm going to die."

"Stubborn girl!" Ma said, mightily annoyed. "I should have given you away like I planned to do."

Zhongmei was shocked into silence by that remark. Growing up, she had always known that her parents, being poor and already having two girls and a boy, had decided before she was born that they would give her to a couple that lived nearby in the village and had no children of their own. But Zhongmei came into the world on December 27, 1966, so small and sickly that her mother had to nurse her for several months, and after she'd done that, looking every day into her new little girl's innocent eyes, she no longer had the heart to give her away.

This story was told often in the Li household. Zhongmei had heard it since she was small. Everybody knew it. And everybody in Baoquanling also knew that the couple that had been slated to become her parents, whose name was Wong and who lived just a few doors down the lane from the Li house, were sorely disappointed when Zhongmei's mother decided to keep her. They had no children and the Lis now had four, and Zhongmei imagined whenever she saw them that they looked at her longingly. Worse, when her mother got angry at her, which didn't happen often but it did happen, she would tell her that the Wongs still wanted her and she could still be given away.

"If you don't behave, I'm going to give you to Mr. and Mrs. Wong," Xiuying would snap.

Zhongmei knew that this wasn't true. It was only her hardworking and hard-pressed mother's way of expressing her annoyance. Still, the idea that the Wongs had hoped to have her embarrassed her and frightened her. It gave her mother's annoyance a special sharpness. Whenever Zhongmei walked past the Wongs' gate, which she did almost every day on her way to school, a kind of nervousness crawled over her skin and she would shiver until she had reached the end of the lane. And now with her hunger strike she had carried disobedience to a new level. Would her mother really give her away this time?

No, Zhongmei said to herself, lying on the *kang*, feeling her hunger like an empty space inside her. Or would she?

"Can I talk to you?"

Zhongmei, who had been facing the wall, turned and watched Lao Lao hobble to the *kang* and sit down next to

27

Zhongmei. She hobbled because she had bound feet. As with many Chinese women of her generation, born near the beginning of the twentieth century when China was still ruled by an emperor, Lao Lao's feet had been wrapped tightly in cloth bands when she was a small girl so their growth would be stunted. Lao Lao had told Zhongmei how horribly painful it was, and that Zhongmei was lucky to be a girl at a time when the practice had stopped. But the custom had been carried out for centuries, because for centuries the Chinese thought tiny feet made a woman desirable. The story of Lao Lao's bound feet fascinated Zhongmei, but it also horrified her and made her indignant. How could people inflict such terrible pain on young girls? It was almost painful just to look at Lao Lao's feet, tiny and curved so that her toes faced backward toward her heel. She could walk, but only very slowly with steps almost as tiny as her feet. It was because of those feet that Zhongmei felt a special tenderness toward her *lao lao*, who seemed to her like a delicate porcelain cup that would shatter in a million pieces if it were rudely handled.

"You know, it's not a good thing what you're doing, this not eating," Lao Lao said.

"Oh, Lao Lao," Zhongmei said. "But nobody will listen to me. What else can I do?"

"Well, you can eat something," Lao Lao said. She gave her granddaughter a conspiratorial look as she took a small bowl of dumplings from behind her back.

Zhongmei looked at her uncertainly.

"Go ahead," Lao Lao said. "Eat. I won't tell anybody."

Zhongmei wolfed the dumplings down, feeling both greedy and guilty.

"Your ma and ba are worried about you," Lao Lao said in her soft voice when Zhongmei was finished.

"Ma told me she's going to give me away to the Wongs," Zhongmei said, "so how much does she really care about me?"

"Oh, you know that's just talk," Lao Lao said. "She loves you very much and she'd never, ever give you away. You can be sure of that."

"If she really cared about me, she'd figure out a way for me to go to the audition."

"Well, let me try to explain to you why that's not exactly right."

Lao Lao had such a sweet way about her that nothing she did could make Zhongmei angry. When she had come from Shandong, she had brought a small statue of the Buddha and a bronze incense burner with her. Such things had been strictly banned during the Cultural Revolution, and even now they certainly weren't encouraged by the government. China's government wanted Chairman Mao to be the country's only god, not the Buddha or Jesus or anybody else. Still, Buddhist shrines at home were permitted. Every morning Lao Lao lit an incense stick, held it in her hand as she bowed to the Buddha, and then placed it in its holder, where it gave an agreeable sandalwood scent to the whole house. Zhongmei had been taught at school that such practices were nothing but old people's superstitions, and maybe they were, but she liked them anyway, and sometimes she asked if she could light an incense stick and bow to the Buddha too. It couldn't do any harm, she figured.

"Your parents are like any other parents," Lao Lao said, "and they care about you a great deal. But do you know how hard they've had to work just so your family could survive?"

"Yes, I know they work very hard," Zhongmei said. She had learned a little about the history of Baoquanling in school, and her mother had told her stories of what it was like in the beginning. Her father had been a soldier in China's army when he was a young man. His whole division, many thousands of men, had been released from the army and sent to this place on the border with Siberia, where almost nobody lived, in order to build it up. When they arrived, there was nothing, hardly any people, no towns, no houses, no electricity, just a vast desolation of thick forests and parched fields.

"It used to be called the Bei Da Huang," Zhongmei said, meaning the Great Northern Wilderness. "They had to cut down the trees and dig out the stumps to make the fields. For a long time the soldiers lived in tents, even in the winter. They had to build a brick kiln to make the bricks so they could build our houses. We learned all that in school. But what does it have to do with whether I can go to the audition in Beijing?"

"Well, this," Lao Lao said. "It seems strange to your mother and father that, after all the work they've done, you're not happy to be here. They're a bit insulted that it doesn't seem good enough for you, and you want them to spend money they don't have to try for something that's probably impossible."

"Well, maybe it is selfish," Zhongmei admitted, "but there

was an advertisement in the newspaper. It said anybody could go as long as they're eleven years old. Lots of girls and boys will go. Why is it selfish if I want to go also?"

"From your point of view that's all very understandable," Lao Lao said.

"Baoquanling is good enough for me," Zhongmei continued, "except I can't be a dancer here, a real dancer."

"Is it your true dream?" Lao Lao asked. "Is it what you want more than anything in the world?"

"Yes," said Zhongmei. Her eyes clouded over. She felt a tear well up in her eye. She didn't mean to think only of herself. She did understand how hard her parents worked—Zhongqin too, who cooked for the whole family and took care of Zhongmei and her younger brother. But did that mean it was wrong for her to have her own dream?

"It's what I want to do more than anything in the world, Lao Lao," Zhongmei said. "And this is my only chance."

"I see," Lao Lao said. She was silent for a minute. Zhongmei looked at the wrinkles around her kind eyes. A few strands of gray hair had fallen out of their clasp and brushed against her cheek.

"Well," Lao Lao resumed, "I'm going to tell you a little story and you can make of it what you will. Do you know the story of how your mother got here?"

"I know she was in Shandong and she got permission from the government to come here after Ba got out of the army."

Shandong is a large province that juts out into the Pacific Ocean far from Heilongjiang.

31

"Yes, that's right," Lao Lao said, "but do you know that she had to walk to get here?"

"She walked?" Zhongmei said, disbelieving.

"And do you know that she had to carry Zhongqin and Zhongling with her?"

Zhongmei didn't know.

"Your mother was living with us at the time, me and Lao Ye, when she got a letter from your father asking her to come here," Lao Lao said. *Lao ye* is the Chinese word for "grandpa." "She wanted to come, but she had no money to buy a train ticket. She asked me and Lao Ye if we could help her with money, and we wanted to, but we didn't have any money either, really none. You may not understand just how poor China was then. A lot of people were starving. They were boiling tree bark and grass to make soup to have something to eat. A train ticket to Heilongjiang seemed like a great luxury.

"This was a few years before you were born. Zhongqin and Zhongling were very small. Zhongling wasn't even a year old yet. So Lao Ye and I told your mother that with two children and no money she had no choice but to stay with us for a while longer until the situation improved.

"But your mother couldn't wait," Lao Lao continued. "She didn't listen to us. She just had to come right away. I remember it so well. She got a bamboo balancing pole. She put Zhongqin in one basket and Zhongling in another basket and she slung the baskets over the two ends of the balancing pole, and what do you think she did next?"

"You just told me, Lao Lao. She walked all the way to Baoquanling."

"Yes, I already told you. She slung the balancing pole over her shoulders and walked to Baoquanling, the two girls bouncing up and down in their baskets. It's a good thing I didn't bind her feet, isn't it, though at the time I wished I had because I thought she was making a terrible mistake. Do you know how far it is from Shandong to here?"

Zhongmei didn't know.

"It's eight hundred miles," Lao Lao said.

"Wow!" It seemed an impossible distance to walk. "Why did you think it was a mistake?" Zhongmei asked.

"Lao Ye and I tried every argument to convince her not to make such a terribly long journey on foot. Your mother didn't even have enough money to buy food along the way. We knew that she was going to have to beg for it. We thought it was dangerous. There were a lot of bad people on the roads in China in those days. There are bad people now too, but there were a lot more of them then. We told her that she could be robbed for the few coins she had. We said, 'The children will starve to death. Even if they don't starve, they'll get sick. Don't be foolish. Just wait a few months. Maybe the situation will change. Maybe Zhengping will be able to send you money for the train in a year or so.'

"But your mother didn't wait. She just put that balancing pole over her shoulders and started walking. For three months we didn't hear any news about her. We were worried sick about all three of them. Then, finally, after a long time, a letter arrived, a very short letter. It said something like, 'I've arrived safely in Baoquanling. Zhengping and the two girls are fine.'"

"Did she really have to walk the whole way?" Zhongmei

asked. Her mother was very small, not five feet tall, less than ninety pounds. Zhongmei knew that she was tough, tough enough to work ten or twelve hours a day in Baoquanling's fields. But to walk eight hundred miles carrying her two babies! The story excited Zhongmei, but it also made her wonder if she was doing the right thing, going on a hunger strike to get what she wanted from parents who had already sacrificed so much.

"From time to time your mother was able to get on a train, but most of the distance she walked, and somehow she made it. But when she got here, your mother was terribly sick," Lao Lao continued. "She had hardly eaten in weeks. Everything nutritious that she was able to beg or steal she gave to the children. She had to be taken to the hospital or she would probably have died. Even now she's not as healthy as she was before."

"Is that why you think I'm doing the wrong thing?" Zhongmei asked Lao Lao.

"I don't know," Lao Lao answered. "Yes, it's selfish of you, I suppose, but there's more than one meaning to every story. Your mother came to Baoquanling even though Lao Ye and I couldn't help her and told her not to do it. At the time we thought her decision was totally wrong and reckless, but in the end she made it. Who knows if she did the right thing? You can only know the result of the things you do, not the things you don't."

"I guess it was the right thing," Zhongmei said, thinking hard. Her mother had defied *her* mother, and now she was defying hers. Was it wrong or was it right? Zhongmei's name was made up of two Chinese characters. There was *Zhong,* pronounced *joong*, which means "faithful," or "loyal," or "filial," as in respectful or obedient to one's parents. The second character, *Mei*, pronounced *may*, is the word for "plum" or "plum blossom," the kind that comes out in the early spring and is a favorite of traditional Chinese painters. So Zhongmei means "faithful plum." But faithful to what? That was the question. Faithful to her parents? Or faithful to her own dream?

"So what do you think I should do?" Faithful Plum asked Lao Lao.

"It's hard to say," Lao Lao said. "But now at least I know what you want."

She patted Zhongmei on the head. "You rest. Let me see what I can do."

Zhongmei lay back, her head on her pillow. She saw her *lao lao* wince as she got off the *kang* and put her small feet on the floor. It hurt her every time she walked. Zhongmei knew that she was fortunate to have nice big feet herself, not the cramped and crippled things some stupid tradition had given to her grandmother for her whole life.

That evening, as she lay on the *kang*, Zhongmei heard someone knocking on the house's front door, and then she heard a voice she recognized talking to her parents. It was the head of their neighborhood in Baoquanling. She couldn't make out the whole conversation, but she heard bits and snatches of it. There was talk of money. She heard her father mention a policeman. Zhongmei didn't know what it meant. She heard her father say, "I don't know if that's such a good idea," and

35

Zhongmei wondered what idea they could be talking about. Was it the idea that she go to Beijing? Her father's voice again: "This hunger strike thing, it's extremely disobedient. If we let her have her way now, isn't it like giving her a reward for behaving badly?"

There was a silence, and Zhongmei thought for a moment that everybody had gone to sleep in the middle of their meeting. Then she heard her *lao lao*'s soft voice.

"Isn't one of the reasons you've worked so hard that you want your children to do things that you couldn't do?" she said. Hearing that brought tears to Zhongmei's eyes. She wanted her heart to stop beating so it would be quiet enough for her to hear more.

But then there was just the murmuring of several voices talking at once. After a while longer, there was a scraping of chairs. And then, still weak from hunger despite Lao Lao's secret dumplings, Zhongmei fell asleep.

4

An Outfit for the Big City

Zhongmei thought about all this as her bus bounced down the road toward Hegang, especially the very end of the story of her hunger strike. As luck would have it the next day was a Sunday, when Zhongmei's parents didn't have to leave the house before dawn. Zhongmei was just rousing herself when her mother came into the room and sat next to her.

"We're going to let you go," she said. Her tone seemed to Zhongmei to be somehow both gentle and annoyed. Light was streaming in through the kitchen window. Zhongmei could smell broth being prepared in the kitchen. Sunday was the day of a special breakfast of noodles in broth with vegetables and, sometimes, chunks of chicken or pork. Her mouth watered at the thought.

"You have Comrade Wu to thank for this," Xiuying said. "Comrade Wu and Lao Lao." Comrade Wu was the head of the neighborhood committee, the man whose voice Zhongmei had recognized the night before. "He's going to help us borrow money for you to take the train to Beijing. We know this is your dream, and we want to give you a chance for it to come true. But you have to promise not to be disappointed if you don't succeed in the auditions, and when you come home, if you ever go on a hunger strike again, we really will give you to the Wongs."

"You will?" Zhongmei said.

"No, of course we won't," her mother said. "But you still have to promise never to go on a hunger strike again."

"I promise," Zhongmei said, her feeling of happiness diminished because she knew she had cheated, eating those dumplings Lao Lao had given her.

"Now get up and eat some noodles," her mother said, heading into the kitchen. She took noodles out of a pot with chopsticks and put them into a blue earthenware bowl, then ladled some broth from the wok. Zhongmei sat in front of the bowl feeling that nothing in her life had ever smelled that good.

"Ba knows somebody in Beijing. His name is Li Zhongshan. He's the policeman who helped him when he went to Beijing to fetch back that silly girl who ran away, and he owes us a favor. He has a son who was living here and wanted to go home, and Ba talked to the leaders and convinced them to let him go. Ba's going to write to him and ask him to take care of you in Beijing."

"Thank you, Ma," Zhongmei said. She leaned over her bowl and felt the steam rising from it tickle her nose and cloud her eyes, or was it something else making her eyes moist like dew? Gratefully she started to eat. Out of the corner of her eye she saw her *lao lao* hobble into the kitchen. She looked at her and smiled, and Lao Lao smiled back.

For the few days before she left, Zhongmei's sisters helped her get ready. They got a bolt of the latest synthetic fabric to arrive at the Baoquanling Department Store, a luxuriant, silky yellow, with plans to make a fancy dress out of it so Zhongmei would fit right in with the sophisticated inhabitants of Beijing. To go with the dress, Zhongqin and Zhongling got Zhongmei the first store-bought shoes she'd had in her life. The department store was like most small-town department stores in China in those days. It was a squat rectangle at the dusty intersection of the town's two big streets and it was filled with pretty dull stuff. There were heavy padded pants and jackets for men and women, either blue or gray or, most commonly, a pale army green, and slightly more colorful padded clothing for children. Unisex shoes were all made out of blue cotton with thin plastic soles or thicker rubber ones, except there was one fashionable-looking pair in the girls' section—green with brown laces—and that's the pair that Zhongqin and Zhongling bought for Zhongmei, even though it was a size too big.

"You'll grow into them in no time," Zhongling, who was always cheerful and optimistic, said.

Zhongmei was overjoyed. She looked over at Zhongqin and Zhongling, appreciating how lucky she was to have two older sisters like that. Since their parents were home so little, it was the older children who were responsible for taking care of the younger ones in the Li household, and so, since she had been a baby, Zhongmei had been raised largely by Zhongqin, with occasional help from Zhongling.

Zhongqin had carried her on her hip just about everywhere she went, even to the Baoquanling Middle School, where she would deposit her younger sister on a little folding stool that she brought with her from home and set next to her desk in the classroom. Sometimes, when she got bored just sitting there and listening to Zhongqin's lessons, Zhongmei would wander to the school entrance and sit on the doorsill there. Sometimes she would play in the school courtyard with children her age who were also being cared for by their older sisters. It got awfully cold in Baoquanling in the winter, so then the children stayed mostly indoors. When Zhongmei was ready for elementary school herself, Zhongqin brought her there in the morning, and picked her up and brought her home in the afternoon. Most important, perhaps, when Zhongmei began taking dance lessons from the young woman who gave them to young children, it was Zhongqin who took her little sister there and picked her up when the lesson was over.

Zhongmei was in the second grade at the time. The children in her class—Young Pioneers all—learned some songs and dances from the Baoquanling Propaganda Brigade, which traveled the whole sprawling state farm and performed for the farmers, sometimes right out in the fields where they were working. The Chinese government in those days wanted everybody, children included, to do songs and dances to celebrate how brave workers and peasants led by Chairman Mao and the

Communist Party defeated evil landlords and foreign invaders and created "the new China." So, like the other children, Zhongmei held a wooden rifle and did a dance with it, crouching as though she were stalking an enemy, lunging forward a couple of steps, then back one, circling counterclockwise before finally springing ahead to shoot some landlord thug in the heart.

A song went with the dance and years later Zhongmei would hum it to herself, not because she liked the lyrics but because of its catchy tune:

> We are sharpshooters,
> One bullet shot,
> One enemy dead.
> We are the soldiers of the revolution.
> No matter how high the mountain,
> Or how deep the river,
> We will make it through.

"You have a very sweet voice," the leader of the Propaganda Brigade told Zhongmei one day.

"Thank you," Zhongmei replied.

Everybody called this young woman Big Xia, but in fact she was very small.

"Would you like to take singing lessons?" Big Xia asked.

"Sure!" Zhongmei said.

"There's a sent-down youth who gives ballet and singing lessons after school," Big Xia told Zhongmei. Years before,

Chairman Mao had ordered millions of students from the big cities to move to villages all over China, sometimes very far away, so they could learn what peasant life was like and help educate the local people. Baoquanling had several of these young people, who were known as the sent-down youth. Some of them got to like countryside life, but many of them felt stuck in remote places for years, their educations interrupted, and they yearned to go home. The girl who ran away and had to be fetched back by Zhongmei's father had fallen in love with a sent-down youth from Beijing who himself had sneaked back home. Some of the members of the Baoquanling Propaganda Brigade were sent-down youths, and so was the ballet teacher who held classes in the primary school for local girls (and a smaller number of boys).

"I'll introduce you to her," Big Xia said.

From then on, once a week Zhongmei went to a small studio in the school to take dance classes. The studio had no barre. Its floor was rough cement, its walls a stained, peeling yellow. The only decorations were the usual color portrait of Chairman Mao and a slogan, square red characters on a white background saying STUDY HARD AND ADVANCE EVERY DAY! There, starting when she was about eight, Zhongmei learned her first curtsies, pliés, and jetés, her inaugural arabesques and battements.

By the time Zhongmei got into the upper elementary school grades, she was deemed to be the prettiest and most talented girl in her class, certainly the best singer, which is the reason she was chosen to perform in front of that microphone in the town hall every day at noon. And every day, there was Zhongqin, escorting her little sister on her rounds. And, naturally enough, it was also Zhongqin who saw that little notice in the *People's Daily* newspaper about the auditions at the Beijing Dance Academy. If it weren't for Zhongqin, Zhongmei realized, she would certainly not be getting ready to go to Beijing.

When the three girls got home from the department store, Zhongling went to work at their mother's sewing machine. A few hours later, after several consultations with Zhongqin, who was busy in the kitchen, she had produced an entire outfit, and her two sisters watched as Zhongmei tried it on. The yellow material had been converted into a pleated yellow skirt coming down below Zhongmei's knees. Wide brown straps crossed over her back and shoulders, and a pink blouse with a curled collar had been added to the ensemble. Green embroidered ducks waddled up and down on either side of the buttons. Zhongmei put on the green shoes with the brown laces, and Zhongling held up a small mirror so she could see herself in her new costume. What she saw was a very slim girl with pigtails in slightly too big clothes, but it didn't matter. Zhongmei had never had anything quite so colorful and elegant. She spun around so the skirt flared out, and gave a shout of joy.

"You look great!" Zhongling said.

"Thank you, Er-jie," Zhongmei said, feeling happy but also a little bit sad. Zhongling was always so eager to please her that sometimes Zhongmei took advantage of it, even a couple of times earning Zhongling a spanking from their mother.

Somehow the beautiful outfit made Zhongmei think about an incident that took place when she was still just a little girl. She was home for a reason she couldn't remember, maybe because she wasn't feeling well, and Zhongling, as she always did when Zhongmei was sick, was taking care of her.

Suddenly Zhongmei declared, "I'm hungry."

There was no food in the house and Zhongling told Zhongmei that she'd have to wait until Zhongqin came home, and then she could go out and buy something at the market.

"I need to eat something now," Zhongmei moaned.

"Well, you're just going to have to wait," Zhongling said.

"I can't stand it," Zhongmei said.

"Well, what do you want me to do? I can't leave you alone to go to the market. You're just going to have to wait. You won't starve."

"But I really can't wait," Zhongmei insisted. "I am starving."

Desperate to stop Zhongmei's suffering, Zhongling went to the back garden to see if she could find something there. Their mother had been working on the garden for weeks. She had planted peas when there was still frost on the ground, but they had already been harvested. The rest of the crop was young. Nothing was ripe, not the eggplants or the scallions or the green beans. But there were two rows of carrots, whose filigree of green shoots was sticking out of the ground. Maybe the carrots underneath are big enough to eat, Zhongling thought. She took hold of the largest of the shoots and pulled it up. A pale carrot-colored thread came out of the ground, a dark skinny thing, more like a rat's tail than an edible vegetable.

"They're too young," Zhongling told Zhongmei, who was standing inside the open backyard door.

"Try that one," Zhongmei said, pointing down the carrot row. "That one looks bigger."

"They're probably all the same," Zhongling pleaded.

"Go ahead, try just one more."

Zhongling pulled out another carrot top, but again there was only the stringy hint of the carrot to come.

"That one over there," Zhongmei shouted, pointing again.

"It's no use," Zhongling protested. "They're too young. Mama will be angry when she sees—"

"I'm starving!" Zhongmei screamed. "Pull that one out!"

"Oh, dear," said Zhongling, eager as she usually was to do something to please her troublesome little sister, and pulling out carrot shoots one by one, hoping to find at least one big enough for Zhongmei to eat. After a few minutes, she had entirely uprooted both rows. Then, seeing the mess she'd made, she spent a desperate half hour trying to reinsert the carrot threads back into their holes. Maybe they can still take root, she thought. She tried her best, smoothing out the soil around the plants when she was done, sprinkling them with water before she went back inside to tend to Zhongmei, who was still loudly demanding food.

The first Sunday after that, Xiuying went into the garden to tend to her plants, and she saw the two rows of torn and wilted carrot heads. She investigated, and Zhongling told her what had happened, getting a good spanking for her mistake, while Zhongmei remained unscathed.

"You're the one screaming at me to tear out the carrots or you'll die of hunger, and I'm the one that gets the beating," Zhongling later told Zhongmei.

"I'm sorry, Er-jie," Zhongmei said. "I was too hungry to think."

Now, wearing the costume that Zhongling had made for her, feeling bad over her lack of appreciation for her wonderful second sister, Zhongmei began to cry.

"What's the matter?" Zhongling asked. "Don't you like the dress?"

"I love it," Zhongmei said. "It's the best thing I've ever had in my entire life."

"Well, what's the matter, then?" Zhongling asked.

"I feel bad because Mama spanked you after you ruined her carrot bed," Zhongmei said as the tears continued to roll down her cheeks. "You were just trying to find me something to eat."

"You're still thinking of that?" Zhongling asked, amazed.

"I feel terrible about it," Zhongmei said, looking down. "You pulled out every carrot and there wasn't a single one to eat."

"Well, I forgive you," Zhongling said, smiling. "I guess."

Zhongqin came into the room from the kitchen. "Life is going to be a lot less trouble with you gone," she said, then, when Zhongmei's face darkened with worry, she hastily added, "Hey! I'm only joking."

"Well, if everybody's right that I have no chance at the audition, I'll be back pretty soon," Zhongmei said, "so you might not have to miss me."

"In that case we'll be happy if you come back and happy if you don't," Zhongqin exclaimed. "What could be better?"

The three sisters' peals of laughter could be heard all the way to the lane outside. They laughed and laughed and laughed and fell into one another's arms.

5

Second Thoughts

*T*he two girls got off the bus in Hegang, which was about the same as Baoquanling, with one large intersection, a few large buildings, and flat, open agricultural fields stretching into the distance. They stood for a while in the dusty station, looking for the bus to Jiamusi. Every once in a while a bus would pull in; other buses pulled out, leaving clouds of stinging blue-gray smoke in their wake.

"There it is!" Zhongqin shouted, and sure enough there was a bus arriving with the Chinese characters for Jiamusi on a placard in the windshield. Jiamusi had marked the farthest point in Zhongmei's travels until now. When she went there before, Zhongmei had thought that Jiamusi was truly a big city. The department store was twice the size of Baoquanling's. Jiamusi had a movie theater, which Baoquanling didn't. Movies in Baoquanling were shown on occasional Saturday nights at a makeshift outdoor theater with a white sheet serving as the screen, which meant that they could only be shown during the warm, mosquito-infested summer months. While Baoquanling consisted of one large intersection, Jiamusi was a real urban grid whose streets were choked with noisy, smoky traffic. Until the idea that she go to the Beijing Dance Academy had come along, Zhongmei's dream had been to settle in Jiamusi and become a member of the song and dance troupe there.

The two sisters had to wait for a few hours in Jiamusi, since the Beijing train didn't leave until early that night. They walked the streets. They ate the cold steamed bread that their mother had prepared for them, dipping it in shrimp paste. Neither of them would ever have thought of going into a restaurant for lunch. Neither of them had ever been inside a restaurant! Zhongmei and Zhongqin looked hungrily at the delicacies on offer at some outdoor food stalls—spiced lamb on skewers, slices of Hami melon, and noodles in soup. Zhongmei looked with particular longing at a stand selling five-fragrance tea-soaked eggs, but she didn't ask Zhongqin to buy one for her. To her, eggs were a very special treat that happened only once a year, on her birthday, when Gao Xiuying gave her a single hard-boiled egg, doing the same for her brothers and sisters on their birthdays. It was the only present any of them would get.

They got only this one egg a year even though the children's mother tended chickens and ducks that produced seven or eight eggs a day right there in the front courtyard. But the eggs weren't for the family. They were a small business that Gao Xiuying ran to earn a little bit of extra money. The first thing she did when she got home from the fields at night was check the roosts and collect the eggs that had accumulated in them, sticking her hand under the bellies of the birds to get at them. But each and every egg had to be sold to help the family survive. Except on birthdays, when everybody got that gift of a single hard-boiled egg.

Zhongmei so treasured hers that she made it last for several days, cutting one thin slice each day and savoring its wondrous mixture of cool, translucent white and dense, mealy yellow. Once she kept her birthday egg in its shell in the pocket of her jacket, waiting for the perfect moment to eat it. After a good long time, maybe two or three weeks, she felt she had waited long enough, and, in a state of tremendous anticipation, she cracked it open. When she peeled away its shell, she noticed a distinctly unpleasant odor emanating from what had turned a kind of greenish purple. The egg had gone sulfurously rotten! Zhongmei's disappointment at missing her once-a-year boiled egg was immeasurable.

Zhongmei had to say good-bye to Zhongqin at the Jiamusi train station, but she didn't have to make the rest of the journey alone. Her parents knew of a young man named Huping, who, like Zhongmei's dance teacher, had spent several years as a sent-down youth in a nearby village. He was now returning home to Beijing, and he was waiting for Zhongmei at the Jiamusi bus station so he could accompany her on the journey. Together they walked across the square from the bus station to the train station. Hundreds of people seemed to be camped out there, sitting with their backs against their bags, even cooking on small coal stoves or just stretched out on the cement, sleeping.

When the train pulled in to the platform, everyone pushed and shoved at the doors to the cars, but Huping lifted Zhongmei up and practically threw her directly through one of the train's windows onto a seat and then dove in behind her. Zhongqin stood on the platform outside their window and gave last-minute instructions. "Don't forget to keep your address in your pocket," she said. "Don't lose your ticket. Make sure you get plenty of pictures in Beijing. I want a picture of you in Tiananmen Square. See everything you can because you may never get another chance to go to Beijing in your whole life. Don't forget the name of Ba's friend who's going to meet you. I've written it down on this piece of paper. Put it in your pocket right away so you won't lose it. Remember you have to change trains in Harbin. You'll arrive there at six in the morning and you have to wait until six that night to get the train to Beijing, so you'll have the whole day in Harbin, but don't wander too far from the train station because you might get lost. Harbin is a big city and there are bad people there. Stay close to Huping and be careful."

With that, Zhongqin thrust two ice sticks that she'd bought on the platform through the window frame, giving one to Zhongmei and the other to Huping. Zhongmei took hers and held it in her hand, hardly noticing it. She was so excited that she'd barely listened to Zhongqin's final instructions. She was off to Beijing! She'd go first thing to Tiananmen, the giant square in Beijing where huge crowds gathered to watch colossal fireworks exhibitions on China's national day. She'd sung a song about Tiananmen often enough on the Baoquanling loudspeakers. Now she'd actually see it! And the Forbidden

City, the vast palace with great curved roofs and marble statues of lions and tall rust-red walls where China's emperors once ruled the country. Beijing had huge theaters, stadiums, parks, and the Great Hall of the People, where the country's leaders had their meetings. It had everything that Baoquanling didn't have, including China's greatest dance academy, to which the country's future stars were summoned. She would see it all, and she would be the first in her family, maybe the only one in her family, to do so!

Suddenly the train shook. It rocked back and forth and then creaked into motion. There was a piercing scream of metal scraping on metal as it began ever so slowly to move forward, and as it did, all of Zhongmei's excitement turned at once into a terrible fear, the inescapable dread of the unknown, which she would have to face without her family, without Zhongling and without Zhongqin, who had been at her side ever since she was born and who was now walking alongside the train trying to keep pace as it gathered speed, shouting good-bye and good luck and have a smooth journey and be sure to write every day!

It was only when the train began to move that Zhongmei fully realized what she had decided to do and what it meant. Instantly she began to miss Baoquanling and all the things she knew of it, their narrow brick house, the little schoolhouse that was so cold in winter that the children wore mittens and earflaps to class, the sound of her own reedy voice carried by loudspeakers at noon over the wheat fields, the *tick tick* of her mother's sewing machine as she made clothes for the family, her friends from her fourth-grade class who teased her about being so skinny, the smell of cabbage at the entrance to her house and the warm broth simmering in the kitchen, the clucking of the chickens and the quacking of the ducks in the front yard, the warmth of the *kang* at night, Lao Lao, the smell of incense burning in front of her statue of Buddha, her mother and father even if she did barely see them, the view of the Heilong River and the distant shore of Russian Siberia on the other side, even Teacher Wang, her fourth-grade teacher, who rapped her ruler on the desk and glared at her when she whispered to her neighbor in class.

Tears now streamed down Zhongmei's cheeks as she thought about it all, blurring her vision so that she could barely see Zhongqin, who had now stopped running but was still standing on the platform waving, getting smaller and smaller as the train picked up speed. It suddenly dawned on Zhongmei that Zhongqin had been right all along, and there really was no chance for her to be chosen at the Beijing Dance Academy. Yes, this whole thing was a stupid act of selfishness and self-delusion. She felt a pang of shame when she thought of her stubbornness, her hunger strike, her family's generosity, and the debt they had incurred to put her on this train, which she was thinking now was carrying her to a place she didn't want to go.

But it was too late for second thoughts. The train was pulling out of the station and picking up speed. It clattered past factories with huge smokestacks, its whistle shrieking to warn pedestrians and bicyclists who waited at intersections behind security gates that flashed red warning lights. There were rows of cement apartment blocks with laundry hanging from bamboo poles on their terraces and open-sided shelters crowded with rows of black Flying Pigeon bicycles. Then, as darkness fell, the wide-open landscape of North Manchuria passed by Zhongmei's window, immense fields bounded by high hills that rose into the sky like the humps of mythological animals. Zhongmei leaned back on her hard seat and readied herself for the long trip.

"Hey, your ice stick is melting!" It was Huping, shaking Zhongmei out of her reverie.

In all the tumult of her mind, she had entirely forgotten to eat the one Zhongqin had thrust through the train window, and it was now dripping syrupy liquid over her hand and onto her blue cotton pants. She licked it, glad to have it, noting that, like this departure for Beijing, it had a distinctly sweet and sour taste.

李忠梅

6

Stranded

Zhongmei and Huping arrived in Harbin after a mostly sleepless night just after dawn the next morning. Harbin was the capital of Heilongjiang, which means "Black Dragon River" and is the northernmost province of China. They had the whole day to wait before their next train, and in the morning they wandered the streets, broader and busier than any Zhongmei had ever seen, but in the afternoon they stayed in the station waiting room, watching the crowds of people surging into the high-ceilinged concourse and out of it again. Outside, through the open station doors, Zhongmei could see a large plaza with groups of people sitting on their bags, lying on the ground and sleeping, taking cigarette after cigarette out of red and white packs labeled DOUBLE HAPPINESS and smoking them while squatting on their haunches. People also smoked in the waiting room, which was filled with an acrid haze. They read newspapers or played cards or Chinese chess, using crinkly plastic sheets for boards and round wooden pieces with the

Chinese characters for "general," "major," "lieutenant," "foot soldier," and "commander-in-chief" printed on them. Across from Zhongmei a man in a well-tailored gray tunic, matching pants, and silver-framed glasses sat and read the *People's Daily*. He had a large metallic watch on his wrist and a black plastic satchel with the characters for Beijing inscribed on it. Zhongmei knew from his refined clothes and watch that he was an official of the government, and she wondered how high up he was.

Finally the time to board their train came. Zhongmei and Huping headed for the hard-seat cars in the rear of the train. Hard seat was the lowest of the three classes of service in China's supposedly classless socialist society. Hard seat meant that they would sit squeezed in among countless others on straight-backed wooden benches, a little like church pews. Above, the luggage racks were crammed with cloth suitcases and red-and-blue-striped plastic bags. In those days, Chinese trains were crowded, dilapidated, uncomfortable, and usually dirty. The next class above hard seat was hard sleeper, which was better than hard seat because there were plastic-covered berths, three levels of them, so passengers were able to lie down, but still it was dingy, smoky, and jammed with people and jumbled with their stuff. The highest class was soft sleeper, but soft sleeper was reserved for high officials, military officers, and the rare foreign visitors who went to China in those days, these privileged passengers enjoying spacious separate compartments each with four comfortable bunk beds, clean white sheets, pillows, and blankets, and large red thermoses full of piping hot tea. But even soft sleeper was hot in summer and freezing in winter, and the other classes of service, hard sleeper and hard seat, were overcrowded all year round. The smells of sweat, garlicky breath, and twice-breathed air were pervasive. All the bathrooms on the train were filthy, dank, and slippery, and they stank horribly. Sometimes they were occupied by passengers who couldn't find room anyplace else. Mothers in hard seat would even let their children pee under the seats, and the smell of children's urine got stronger as the trip stretched from hours to days. Zhongmei was too old to do that, so she tried hard not to go, until she just couldn't wait any longer, and then it was a matter of balancing on treacherously slimy footrests while squatting over a metal-rimmed hole, clinging to a small bar alongside to avoid being thrown to the disgusting floor when the train lurched.

For much of the time between Harbin and Beijing, Zhongmei sat between two men with patchy beards, rough blue clothes, and breath sour from the smell of pickled garlic. From time to time one or the other of them would hawk noisily and spit on the floor between his feet. At night her fellow passengers slept in their seats sitting straight up, their heads thrown back, their mouths agape, showing blackened teeth and snoring loudly, but Zhongmei was both too excited and too uncomfortable to sleep much at all.

But at least she was sitting. Huping, who didn't get a seat, gallantly stood in the aisle or squatted on his haunches for the entire twenty-four-hour trip. At every stop there was a mad commotion as more and more people tried to get on the train. Vendors would lean into the train's open windows trying to sell various edibles—peanuts, roasted corn on the cob, plastic packages of crackers, balls of cold steamed rice wrapped around dollops of sweet red bean paste, bottles of Chrysanthemum-brand orange soda pop, which Zhongmei coveted but didn't drink because there was no money for such delicacies. Anyway, by not drinking soda pop, she wouldn't have to go to the terrible toilet so often. When the train started up again, the vendors would run with it, reaching into the cars for the money for their final sales.

Sometime after midnight Zhongmei managed to doze off, wedged as she was between her fellow passengers, but she woke up frequently when, for some reason, the train would just stop, and the mesmerizing *clickety-clack* of its movement would be replaced by the overpowering silence of China's vast, dark, and lonely countryside. The train would sit for a long time, the interior lit by a ghostly yellow light coming from the weak lamps on the ceiling above. The sounds of snoring and the murmuring of voices seemed louder than before, but it was only because the train itself had become so quiet. Zhongmei tried to look out the streaked and stained windows beyond her seat to see what was outside, but nothing was visible but her own dim reflection.

Why isn't the train moving? she asked herself. This was the second night on a train, and she longed to be able to lie flat someplace and sleep like she did every night on the *kang* back in Baoquanling. Her back hurt, her neck was stiff. Would this mournful journey ever end?

Zhongmei looked over at Huping in the aisle. He was squatting in the aisle and leaning forward, his head against the edge of the seat in what must have been a very uneasy sleep. Finally, after what seemed to Zhongmei a long time, there was a jolt and a grinding of metal on metal and the train creaked forward again.

Daybreak was marked by a few bars of bombastic music over the train's scratchy loudspeakers, and then a dulcet female voice. "Comrades," it said, "please pay attention to security and safeguard your possessions. Hygiene is very important. Cover your mouth when you cough, don't spit or throw trash on the ground, be polite to your fellow passengers, and work hard to build our socialist motherland."

Zhongmei was used to these morning loudspeaker broadcasts. They were the same as the ones that awakened her parents every morning in Baoquanling. China had spent more than one hundred years in very poor and humiliating conditions. For decades the country was divided among warlords, who spent their time fighting each other. Its biggest cities were controlled by foreign countries; during the long, devastating years of World War II, when Zhongmei's parents were children, the whole country was under constant attack by Japan. Almost twenty years before Zhongmei was born, the revolutionaries led by Chairman Mao had taken power. They eliminated the warlords, and the foreign armies were gone. China now was still poor, and it was certainly not free. Those who expressed any criticism of Chairman Mao especially would find themselves quickly in a large, remote prison camp, where they would spend a few years in what was called reform through labor. Everybody was called on to obey the government and to work hard for low wages, until the country was rich and strong again. That's what all those morning broadcasts were about. That's what the songs Zhongmei sang at noon in Baoquanling were about, and the revolutionary dances as well, millions of Chinese children armed with wooden rifles and pretending to shoot the enemy dead.

But around the time Zhongmei took her trip to Beijing, all of this was just on the point of changing. Chairman Mao had died two years earlier. Mao's closest backers had been arrested and put in jail and a new group of leaders was now in place and wanted China to calm down, to be a little less revolutionary and a bit more normal. The schools reopened, teachers who had been exiled to the countryside were allowed to come back, and so were sent-down youths like Huping. China was becoming more relaxed. People were being allowed to do more of the things they wanted to do without supervision, like falling in love, getting married, or, like Lao Lao, building little shrines to Buddha. Before, if you asked young people what they wanted to do when they grew up, they would all reply, "We want to be good soldiers of our great leader Chairman Mao and build the world revolution!" Now they could freely say they wanted to be teachers, or scientists, or dancers, and they didn't have to say anything about Chairman Mao at all. That doesn't mean he wasn't all over the place, in pictures and statues. Everybody was still entreated almost every day to "work hard to build the new China." Nobody was allowed to criticize the country's new leaders. And there were, as always, all those loudspeakers, though the message was no longer "Fight, struggle, annihilate the enemy!" but "Please don't spit; clean up after yourselves."

At about eight o'clock that morning, the train arrived in Shenyang, the capital of Liaoning Province, which signaled to Zhongmei that for the first time in her life she had ventured beyond the borders of Heilongjiang Province. A voice on the loudspeaker announced that the train would stop for half an hour, so Huping ran across the platform to buy some breakfast dumplings. Zhongmei fretted while he was gone, worried that the train would leave before he got back, certain that she would lose her precious seat if she left it to go look for him. She kept her eyes on the platform, trying to find him among the crush of passengers and vendors. A troop of soldiers in green uniforms with red collar tabs and visored hats marched by her window. Mothers held small children over the tracks on the other side of the platform, their pants, ingeniously slit at the crotch, opening so they could relieve themselves.

The time went by and still there was no Huping. The man sitting next to her leaned out the window, cleared his throat, and spat onto the platform, making Zhongmei want to ask him if he hadn't heard the announcement about politeness and hygiene just a while before, but she kept quiet. A vendor bearing trays of roasted chestnuts stood at the window and looked at Zhongmei expectantly, but she shook her head. And then, suddenly, there was Huping smiling happily at the window and handing Zhongmei a thin clear plastic bag of warm steamed-bread dumplings filled with chopped cabbage and noodles, which she gratefully devoured.

The train resumed its march toward Bejing, passing Fuxin,

61

Beipiao, Jianing, Pingquan, and Miyun, Zhongmei getting excited as she read the signboards on the stations, naming places that she'd never heard of before. China was so big, who could know it all? The countryside was flat now. Zhongmei could see the outlines of mud-brick villages on the horizon, marked by clumps of plane trees, gray birches, and locusts. Tree-lined roads extended away from the tracks, crowded with wagons and carts drawn by men on bicycles or by teams of oxen, just like the ones back home. Great mounds of hay dotted some of the fields. Others were filled with neat straight rows of beans, mustard greens, and cabbages. Groups of farmers leaned on their hoes and watched as the train went by. From time to time the train would cross a trestle bridge, which amplified the *clackety-clack* of the wheels as if somebody had opened a window to let the sound in.

At the end of the afternoon just as dusk began to fall, the train rumbled past a kind of suburban sprawl. Zhongmei saw row after row of brick factory buildings with round chimneys issuing forth great plumes of black smoke. There were piles of cinder blocks and steel reinforcement rods, and an endless succession of barracks and sheds, brick kilns and piles of gravel, then gray cement apartment blocks with the usual rows of bicycles parked under tarpaulin-covered sheds in front of them and laundry hung out to dry on tiny balconies on every floor. Every building, every wall, seemed to be inscribed in large Chinese characters with one of the slogans of those days—STRIVE FOR EVER GREATER VICTORIES! LET'S RELY ON OURSELVES ONLY! RESOLUTELY BUILD A RADIANT SOCIALIST FUTURE! The train went past road junctions, and Zhongmei saw what seemed like thousands of people on bicycles jammed up behind security gates, all of them, men and women, dressed in identical blue jackets and trousers.

Then there were glimpses of grand-looking buildings, wide avenues, big statues, streetlamps, and photographs of Chairman Mao. The train, running now on an elevated platform, offered a view of countless interior courtyards, each of which had a large red tablet inscribed with the slogan SERVE THE PEOPLE in the scrawled calligraphy that everybody knew was Chairman Mao's. Finally the train pulled beneath a large canopy of leaded glass and came to a stop. Zhongmei saw the characters BEIJING mounted on a red signboard. They had arrived! She and Huping gathered their things and joined the throng as it pushed toward the platform, over a bridge, and then down into the terminal building.

Zhongmei had never seen anything so vast or so crowded. High, grimy windows allowed feeble slants of light into the immense hall, which teemed with people, some rushing about, many more just camped out on the floor or leaning against pillars and walls smoking the inevitable Double Happiness cigarettes, surrounded by suitcases and striped plastic bags. There were long lines of people buying tickets or waiting to get onto platforms. Zhongmei and Huping stood in the middle of the hall hoping that they would be seen by the two people they were expecting to meet them, Li Zhongshan and Huping's mother.

After a few minutes, Huping's mother arrived. She took

one look at her son, whom she hadn't seen in years, and burst into tears of joy. Naturally, she wanted to take Huping home right away. His father was waiting for them there, she said. But first they had to be sure that somebody came for Zhongmei, and so far nobody had. The three of them waited amid the commotion of the station. The time passed. Thousands of people continued to push by. There were announcements over the loudspeaker, but the words were so lost in the vastness of the great hall that they could scarcely be understood. Anyway, Zhongmei was so eager to find her father's friend, or to be found by him, that she didn't really listen to them. Of course, she didn't know what Li Zhongshan looked like, only that he was a policeman, so every time a policeman came near, Zhongmei would stand up straight and make herself as visible as she could. But no policeman or anybody else took any notice of her at all.

7

An Amazing Coincidence

The windows of the station waiting room darkened as the light in Beijing began to fade. What could have happened to Policeman Li? Before Zhongmei left home, her father had sent his friend an old picture of Zhongmei. In China in those days, few people from the countryside could afford cameras or film, and having their picture taken was a rare and special event that took place in a photo studio, which meant that the picture Zhongmei's father sent to Li Zhongshan was taken when Zhongmei was about seven years old. It showed Zhongmei as a very little girl, her bangs down to her eyes, and a gauzy scarf around her neck, and while she was now a good deal bigger, the eleven-year-old Zhongmei could still be discerned in the picture of the seven-year-old Zhongmei. Unbeknownst to Zhongmei, Policeman Li did come to the station, but he didn't find Zhongmei. Maybe he looked for a girl exactly like the one in the photograph, and Zhongmei wasn't that girl anymore.

"What can we do?" Huping's mother asked.

"You go ahead home," Zhongmei said bravely, even though she wasn't feeling very brave. "I'll wait here. I'm sure he'll come. You don't have to worry about me." But she wanted very much for them to worry about her.

"If he was going to come, he'd have been here long ago," Huping's mother said. "It's pointless to wait any longer. You better come home with us."

Zhongmei looked around the station, which reverberated with noises and echoes, with a thousand shouts and murmurs, with the scraping of luggage being dragged across the floor, with the wailing of babies, with public announcements that seemed to be swallowed up by the very vastness of the place. The station was less crowded than before, less filled with rushing people, and Zhongmei stayed anchored to her spot, thinking that she'd now be easier to see. But nobody came, and, as the hall continued to empty, Zhongmei had the feeling that nobody would. But for Huping's family, she was alone in China's immense capital, and the person who had vowed to take care of her had vanished.

She went home with Huping's family. Huping's mother's surname was Chen. Zhongmei called her Chen Aiyi, Auntie Chen, and his father Shu-shu, Uncle. She gratefully accepted their hospitality, knowing that if it wasn't for them, she would have been out on the streets like a beggar. She had food to eat and a roof over her head, and the family was nice. Nonetheless, she wondered what to do. It wasn't going to be a simple thing to find Policeman Li. Unlike today in China, she couldn't just flick on her cell phone and give her parents a call to find out Li Zhongshan's address. Almost nobody in China had a home telephone in those days, much less a cell phone. On the rare occasion when they did make private calls, they used telephones tended by shopkeepers on the streets, paying a few fen per call. And in the entire country of one billion people there were no telephone books, so she couldn't simply look up Li Zhongshan and get his number and address that way. Zhongmei could have written a letter to her father telling him to write to Li Zhongshan and give him the address of Huping's family, where he could come to fetch her, but by the time all that could be done, the audition, which was to start in just a few days, would already be over.

"Don't worry," Chen Aiyi said. "I'm sure we'll find this Policeman Li, or he'll find you. My husband is going to go to the main police station on his day off from work to ask about him."

But Zhongmei did worry. For hours she sat at the family's house, which was actually a part of a larger house built in three sections around a narrow courtyard. An imposing entry gate of carved wood led from the lane into the courtyard. The rooms had large windows covered by lattices of dark wood. The roofs were of gray tile. Water came from a pump with a curved metal handle painted red in the middle of the courtyard. This courtyard was a crowded place, since lots of small rooms made out of cinder blocks or bricks with corrugated metal roofs had been put up next to the older ones, and it was crammed with stuff—crates for storing cabbage, sheds with cooking pots, plates, cups, teapots, and enamel basins for washing. Here and there were braziers for cooking, piles of coal-dust bricks that were used in the braziers, washtubs and corrugated scrubbing boards for doing laundry, a flotsam and jetsam of discarded pieces of furniture. Two pomegranate trees grew there as well, and small green fruits were beginning to take shape on their branches. Ropes suspended from hooks in the houses crisscrossed the yard and were used to dry the laundry that was done in the outdoor washtubs, using water drawn from the pump. As in Baoquanling, the toilet was a public one down the lane. So was the bath, where Chen Aiyi took Zhongmei on her first night to wash off the dust of her long journey.

"This used to be a rich family's house," Chen Aiyi told Zhongmei as they came back to the courtyard, carrying their towels and a dish of soap, wearing fresh clothing, "but after the revolution, the place was divided up so some poor people could come live here, including us."

"Is the rich family still here?" Zhongmei asked.

"Oh, yes," Chen Aiyi said. "They're in that room over there." She pointed across the courtyard. "They're just an old couple. Their children left years ago. But we don't see much of them. They don't mix with us."

Zhongmei was amazed that this part of Beijing wasn't all that different from Baoquanling. Indeed, her house in Bao-quanling, which was also down a narrow lane, was small, narrow, and dark, but it was bigger than the portion of the courtyard house that her new Beijing family occupied. Zhong-mei slept on a narrow cot pushed against the whitewashed wall of the living room, while Aiyi and Shu-shu slept in a bed in the other half of the same room, which was blocked off by a screen made of pleated red cloth. But she didn't sleep well. There was a lot of noise in the courtyard until late at night. Zhongmei could hear conversations, laughter, and infants crying in the neighboring rooms. One of Huping's parents—was it Aiyi or Shu-shu? Zhongmei couldn't tell—snored loudly.

But even if Chen Aiyi's house was modest and crowded, it was pretty different from Baoquanling. Intricate, delicate latticed woodwork covered the large windows, and the floor was of polished wood, not the cement of Zhongmei's hometown. In the Chen living room, there was a large scroll painting showing a scene of mountains, forests, waterfalls, and winding paths, along which a monk in rust-brown robes, looking very small in the surrounding immensity of nature, rode on a donkey. On the steep, craggy hills above the man were pavilions with carved railings and sloping roofs. Nobody in Baoquanling had a painting like that. In Baoquanling, people had portraits of Chairman Mao or revolutionary posters showing farmers marching under a bright red sun into the fields, holding pitchforks in one hand, copies of a little red book of Mao quotations in the other. By contrast, the painting in this house in Beijing suggested to Zhongmei something deeper, quieter, more elegant; something very refined and civilized.

Also, after just a day or so, Zhongmei noticed that the people in Beijing were different. They had smooth, pale faces. Many of them wore store-bought white or printed cotton shirts and blouses and leather shoes. The farmers that Zhongmei grew up with seemed grizzled and leathery by comparison, or the men did. The women in Baoquanling had ruddy complexions, made that way by the sun and the wind. They wore threadbare, patched clothing and cotton shoes with plastic or rubber soles mostly made at home. After only a day in Beijing, Zhongmei saw something she'd never seen in Baoquanling—a beauty parlor. It was just down the lane from Chen Aiyi's house. Inside, a row of women sat under machines that covered their heads, and when they extracted themselves from this device, their hair was curly and lustrous. Next to the beauty parlor was a photo studio, in the window of which were sample pictures of people in very fancy clothing, young women with that beauty-parlor hair and frilly white dresses standing next to men in dark jackets and white shirts against backgrounds of mysterious purple swirls, as if a heavy storm raged just behind them. In Beijing, Zhongmei saw young men wearing wraparound sunglasses, with small oval labels printed in a foreign language stuck to the outside of the lenses. There were no dark glasses in Baoquanling. There, when the sun was too bright, people just squinted.

Dear Da-jie, Zhongmei wrote to Zhongqin, sitting in her bed on her second night in Beijing, using a pen and a piece of paper Chen Aiyi had given her.

> I miss you, but everything's OK. Policeman
> Li didn't meet me at the station, so I'm staying
> with Huping's family. That was a surprise.
> Beijing is big and kind of scary. I don't know why
> Policeman Li didn't come for me. Maybe they
> changed their mind about letting me stay at their
> house. Don't tell Ma and Ba. I don't want them
> to worry. I don't want you to worry either.
> > Your sister Zhongmei

That night, Zhongmei sat up for a long time in her bed, looking out the window and thinking. Across the courtyard, in front of the former owner's room, she could see somebody sitting in a straight-backed chair. A cigarette glowed in the dark and reflected in the lenses of glasses of a person who was otherwise just a dark shape in the shadows.

Why, oh why, had she made this journey? she thought. How was she going to get to the auditions if Policeman Li didn't find her, and how was he going to find her in this big city? Chen Aiyi told Zhongmei not to worry, but what explanation could there be for his not turning up at the train station, other than that he didn't want her anymore? The information about the train that Zhongmei's family had sent ahead had been entirely accurate, and the train had arrived on time. And anyway, Li Zhongshan was a policeman. He was just the kind of person who ought to be able to find somebody arriving at the Beijing train station, and if he hadn't found Zhongmei, it must be because he didn't want to find her. That was very mean, Zhongmei thought, very unkind. Policeman Li and his wife must have known that Zhongmei had nowhere else to go, and yet he hadn't shown up. Maybe that was the way people behaved in Beijing. Nobody in Baoquanling would ever act like that, she felt.

The first day in Beijing, Huping had taken her for a walk around the neighborhood, which was one of Beijing's oldest. The family's lane was called Da Shi Qiao Hutung, which means "Big Stone Bridge Lane," and it led to a street called Old Drum Tower Street, which was crowded with small shops selling

71

ready-made clothing, bolts of cotton and woolen cloth, enameled basins, Golden Bridge toothpaste and Bee and Flower soap, along with framed pictures of Chairman Mao, the *People's Daily* newspaper, *Red Flag* magazine, and coal-dust bricks for cooking. A particularly fascinating shop displayed shelf after shelf of clear glass jars of medicinal roots, curled-up snakes, and the gall bladders and hearts of rabbits, civet cats, and other animals. On a counter were bowls of powdery substances, including (or so the sign proclaimed) tiger bone and rhinoceros horn, and dried mountain herbs and grasses that, steeped in a tea, were believed effective against rheumatism, arthritis, heart disease, cancer, fatigue, anemia, and nightmares.

Old Drum Tower Street rang to the sound of a million bicycle bells and the occasional clang of a streetcar bell, because old green electrical streetcars still ran there, connecting the Dongcheng District with the center of Beijing. Despite her worries, Zhongmei loved walking down narrow Big Stone Bridge Lane to Old Drum Tower Street and gazing at the passing throngs, more people every hour than you'd see in Baoquanling in a month. After a day, Huping went away to visit his grandparents, whom he hadn't seen since he'd been sent down to the countryside years before, and that left Zhongmei alone during the day, since both Aiyi and Shu-shu had to work. So every day she took a walk around the neighborhood, thinking about her situation.

Old Drum Tower Street led to a massive structure called, not surprisingly, the Drum Tower. It was a six-hundred-year-old building that had formed part of the massive wall that surrounded the entire city when the emperors of China's past lived there, and Zhongmei thought it was the most magnificent thing she had ever seen. It was enormously tall and wide, but it didn't seem heavy. In fact, it seemed to soar. A set of stone steps led up to a tall red-painted foundation, above which were three sets of curved roofs, one atop each of the tower's floors, with each floor marked by an ornate latticed railing, and the whole thing surmounted by a roof that curved upward into the sky.

Lots of people visited the Drum Tower, and Zhongmei could see them standing and looking out at Beijing from behind one or another of the upper railings. She read the information placard at the Drum Tower gate, which informed her that in ancient times the drum had sounded every hour to keep people informed of the time. But the entry ticket cost ten fen, and Zhongmei didn't feel right about spending the money.

No, she would have to save every penny of the small sum her parents had given her for the journey. Walking was free and enjoyable, but there could be no paid-for small pleasures, not even a ride on the electric streetcar, which would take her to some of Beijing's other great monuments. That would have to wait. Zhongmei simply walked around, circling the Drum Tower several times, looking up at it, enjoying its delicate power. She cut a small and lonely figure, her head bent as she contemplated her situation, so far from home and so seemingly hopeless. She was furious at Policeman Li for not having come for her at the train station. She was angry at her father for having chosen so unreliable a person to care for her, somebody who manifestly didn't want to care for her. She missed her friends, her brothers and sisters, especially Zhongqin, who had always been at Zhongmei's side and now was so far away.

Zhongmei squatted in front of the Drum Tower gate and traced lines in the dust with a twig. People came and went, people she didn't know, people who paid no attention to her. In Baoquanling, she knew everybody and everybody paid attention to her.

> Dear Da-jie,
>
> I realize now what I'm going to do. Huping's family is very nice. I'm going to ask them if I can stay with them for the audition. They can show me how to take the bus to the Beijing Dance Academy, so I can go by myself. Probably I won't get chosen. Then I'll be able to visit the famous places in Beijing and come back to Baoquanling and never leave it again.

Having composed this letter to Zhongqin in her head, Zhongmei got up and made her way back to the house, intending to write it down and send it off right away.

But when she arrived at the entrance to Big Stone Bridge Lane, Chen Aiyi was waiting, excited about something.

"Ah, there you are!" she exclaimed. "I've been waiting for you. I have something to tell you, something amazing."

Zhongmei was so surprised, she was speechless.

"Let's walk home together and I'll tell you as we go," Chen Aiyi said, and she embarked on a confusing story, which Zhongmei didn't understand at first.

"I've known this for a couple of days, but I didn't want to tell you until I was sure," Chen Aiyi said.

"Didn't want to tell me what?" Zhongmei asked impatiently.

"That I found Policeman Li!" Chen Aiyi said.

"You found Policeman Li?"

"Well, not exactly."

"Oh," said Zhongmei.

"I didn't find Policeman Li, but I found his wife. She's very nice, and I'm sure Policeman Li is nice too. They've been so worried since they couldn't find you, but now they have, or, I should say, I've found them, but it doesn't matter. What matters is that Policeman Li is coming for you today!"

"He is?" Zhongmei was happy, but she was also nervous. She had built up such an unfavorable opinion of Policeman Li during the past couple of days that she wasn't sure she really wanted to meet him anymore.

"Yes," Chen Aiyi was saying. "His wife works in the same factory as me. Isn't that amazing? Such a big city, Beijing, millions of people, so many factories, and we work in the same one! I found out because after you arrived and I went to work, I told some of my co-workers that there was this girl from Heilongjiang and she's come to Beijing for the dance auditions, and nobody had come to pick her up at the train station, so she was staying with me."

Chen Aiyi paused to catch her breath.

"Well," she resumed. "The day before yesterday, somebody I know told me that she heard there was another woman at the factory who was also talking about a girl from Heilongjiang. This other woman said that she was looking for her. Naturally, at first I thought there must be lots of girls from Heilongjiang, so I didn't think much of it, but then yesterday my friend told me that the other woman's husband was a policeman! She works in a different part of the factory from me. I went to see her during my rest break. The woman had a picture of the girl they were looking for. It was taken some time ago, but as soon as I saw it, I knew it was you!"

Chen Aiyi stopped and smiled at Zhongmei. They were just outside the gate to their courtyard.

"But what if they don't want me?" Zhongmei asked.

"What if who doesn't want you?"

"Policeman Li and his family," Zhongmei exclaimed. "He didn't meet me at the train station. Maybe they don't want to take care of me."

"Of course they want you," Chen Aiyi said. "Just go in and get ready. He's going to be here very soon."

Zhongmei, reassured but still not certain that finding Policeman Li would turn out to be a good thing, scampered into the house and quickly put her few things into her small cloth suitcase, rushing so much that she didn't even bother to fold the city outfit Zhongqin and Zhongling had made for her but just stuffed it in. She grabbed the suitcase and ran out to the courtyard. She looked out into the lane in anticipation of the man in a policeman's uniform who would soon materialize.

She saw no walking policeman, only a large man on a motorcycle slowly navigating the potholes of Big Stone Bridge Lane. As he got closer, Zhongmei realized that he was wearing a policeman's uniform, green with red shoulder tabs and a large visored hat that came down to his eyes.

"Zhongmei?" the man said, speaking over the rumbling sound of the motorcycle engine.

"Policeman Li?"

"I'm so glad to find you!" Policeman Li said. "I'm so sorry! We've been worried to death about you. I don't understand how this could have happened, because I went to the train station on the day you arrived, and I looked all over, but I just didn't find you. I even had the station master make an announcement over the public address system. They called your name and asked you to go to the number one ticket window. I waited there a long time but you never came."

Zhongmei remembered the incomprehensible public address announcements reverberating in the vastness of the Beijing train station.

"I didn't understand the announcements," Zhongmei said. "I was just standing there, waiting for you."

"Well, why didn't I see you there?"

"How should I know?"

"It's a mystery," Policeman Li said. He was a large man with a big belly and kindly eyes. Looking at him, Zhongmei began to like him. "Da-ma will be so happy," he said. *Da-ma* means "big mother." It's a standard form of address in China for an older woman who is actually not your mother. Policeman Li was talking about his wife. "She's been scolding me every day since I didn't find you at the train station. 'How could you not find her?' she's been saying. 'How many eleven-year-old girls traveling by themselves could there have been?' And she's right. I looked everyplace. I just don't understand how it was that I didn't see you."

"I was worried you didn't want me anymore," Zhongmei said. This was the girl, after all, still haunted by all those threats, casually muttered over the years, to give her away to another family. If her own family wasn't sure they wanted her, how could she be sure that Policeman Li's family would?

"What do you mean?"

"Well, when you didn't come for me at the train station, I figured you didn't want me to come to your house," Zhongmei explained.

"What sheer nonsense!" Policeman Li said. "Da-ma has talked about nothing besides you for a week. I'm glad we'll be able to talk about something else now." He smiled and turned to Chen Aiyi, who was standing in the entryway watching and smiling.

"If you don't mind, comrade, I'm going to take her home now. My wife is waiting impatiently. Thank you for your help."

"You're welcome," said Chen Aiyi. "Zhongmei," she said, "please come to see us before you go back to Baoquanling."

"I will," Zhongmei said happily, feeling suddenly lighter than before, the weight of her worries lifted from her shoulders.

"Have you ever ridden one of these before?" Policeman Li said, nodding at his police-issue motorcycle. "No? Well, climb on behind and hold on to me."

Policeman Li turned his motorcycle around and drove slowly out of the lane. Zhongmei turned and waved to Chen Aiyi, who was still standing at the courtyard gate. Policeman

Li turned the motorcycle down Old Drum Tower Street and picked up speed. They passed bicycles, trucks, and streetcars. When they roared past the Drum Tower, Zhongmei suppressed the urge to wave at it, as at an old friend. She felt the wind in her face and her hair blowing behind her.

"I'll take you past Tiananmen!" Policeman Li shouted. "Have you been there yet?"

"No," shouted Zhongmei. She was still a little scared on the back of the motorcycle and wrapped her arms around Policeman Li, but he was so big that her arms didn't reach all the way around. They were in the middle of the widest street Zhongmei had ever seen. Soon, looming into view was an expanse of asphalt so vast it seemed to fade almost to the horizon. At one end was a great red wall and a massive gate surmounted by the same kind of curved tile roofs she'd seen at the Drum Tower. Three arched marble bridges led over a moat and toward the massive, imposing gate that was the entrance to the Forbidden City, where China's emperors had once lived. Behind, Zhongmei could see the green-tiled curved roofs of numerous palatial buildings. In front, just above the gate, was a picture of Chairman Mao.

Tiananmen! In those days every child was told that the most exciting thing that could happen to any Chinese person was to visit Tiananmen, and now Zhongmei was there! How quickly things had changed. A few hours ago she was disconsolately scratching the earth with a twig; now she was flying on the back of a policeman's motorcycle through Tiananmen Square!

"Look over there," Policeman Li said, pointing to a large rectangular building with a sort of orange frieze. A long line of people led up to it. Zhongmei knew what it was. She had seen pictures of the mausoleum where Chairman Mao's body was preserved in a glass case.

"And that over there is the Great Hall of the People," Policeman Li said, pointing to another immense building that Zhongmei recognized, the place where China's government held its important national meetings.

Zhongmei was indescribably excited.

> Dear Da-jie,
> I saw Tiananmen Square today. It's even bigger than I imagined it. I'm now living with Policeman Li's family. He's very nice. Da-ma is nice too. When I walked into the house, the first thing she did was rush up to me and throw her arms around me like I was her daughter. She told me a thousand times how angry she was at Policeman Li because he couldn't find me at the train station. They have one son.
> Tomorrow he's going to take me to the Forbidden City and he'll take lots of pictures that I'll show you when I get home, because he works in a photographic studio. The audition starts the day after tomorrow. Policeman Li is taking me on his motorcycle. I know now that I'm not going to get into the Beijing Dance Academy. But it's OK. I saw Tiananmen. I'm happy.
>
> Zhongmei

李忠梅

8

Taking Measurements

*Z*hongmei made a grand entrance on the first day of the auditions, arriving at the Beijing Dance Academy on the back of a motorcycle driven by a stout policeman in uniform. But soon Li Zhongshan had to go to the police station, and as the rumble of the motorcycle receded into the distance, she found herself very much alone.

"That's the Dance Academy," Policeman Li had said, pointing at a black wrought-iron gate. Behind it was a set of three-story buildings around an asphalt courtyard. "Just go in there and tell them who you are. I'll be back for you tonight at six o'clock."

Zhongmei stood at the entryway. A brass sign with black Chinese characters marked it as the Beijing Wu-dao Xue-yuan, the Beijing Dance Academy. She was wearing the costume her sisters had made for her, the yellow skirt, pink blouse with the embroidered ducks, and green shoes with the brown laces, and she was ready to show what a good dancer she could be. But where to go? Who should she tell that she was there? Crowds of people were gathered outside the gate; another crowd milled about in the courtyard within. There were lots of girls and boys Zhongmei's age, and they all seemed to be accompanied by parents, brothers and sisters, grandmothers and grandfathers, all except Zhongmei. She had the feeling that all of them except her knew what to do. She tried to push her way past the gate into the courtyard to try to get to the entrance to the school, but there were too many people. The way was blocked. She stood there helplessly.

"Form a line! Form a line!" a voice shouted after what seemed like a long time. A man with a handheld loudspeaker stood on the steps of one of the buildings inside the courtyard, a cream stucco edifice lined with rectangular windows.

"Boys on the left; girls on the right," he said. "Form a line and wait your turn to register."

But there was no line. There was just a crush of people pressing vaguely toward the school entrance, plus the thousands of people outside on the street, pressing toward the gate. Zhongmei was among them.

"You people outside the gate," the man with the loudspeaker shouted. "Form a line next to the wall and down the block. Please be orderly. Please be considerate. Please wait your turn and everybody will be given a chance to register."

It took a long time. A bunched and ragged line did eventually form. It went down the small street that the gate opened onto and then turned the corner down a much larger street, across from which was the entrance to a park. Zhongmei found herself near the end of the line, way down the big street, a long distance from the gate. The time passed. Slowly she inched forward. Cars, trucks, buses, and a very large number of bicycles flowed by indifferently. There was a lot of honking mixed with the tinkling of bicycle bells. Whenever a bus or truck went by, vapors of exhaust would wash over the people in the line. It was a hot day, but at least the sidewalk was lined by a row of locust trees that gave the crowd of Dance Academy hopefuls some relief from the bright sun. At around noon, four hours after arriving on Policeman Li's motorcycle, Zhongmei turned the corner. An hour later she reached the gate. She ate a steamed bun and an apple that Policeman Li's wife had packed for her that morning. Two hours after that, she found herself on the pavement in front of the door to the school itself. Tables had been set up at the entrance outside, one for the boys and one for the girls, where a harried, perspiring woman in a plain white blouse handed her a piece of paper on which she filled in blanks asking for her name, her identity card number, and her home address.

The woman looked over the form when Zhongmei handed it back to her and raised her eyebrows.

"You've come a long way," she said as she recorded Zhongmei's information in a large ledger on the table in front of her. "Go to studio eleven. It's that way," the woman said, gesturing toward the door of the school. "Up the stairs, third floor. Give them this," she said, and she handed Zhongmei a card with her name and a number on it.

Zhongmei walked through the door. It was the first time she set foot into what was to become her home for the next eight years, though she didn't know that yet. Before she left

Baoquanling, Zhongmei had prepared a little dance, getting help from her ballet teacher. It was a two-minute solo part from *The Red Detachment of Women*, and as she walked up the two flights of stairs to studio eleven Zhongmei rehearsed it in her mind. Her moment was coming! She knew the odds were against her, but she was determined to dance well, to try to impress the judges.

She found studio eleven, where a young woman—she couldn't have been more than twenty—took her card.

"Stand by the wall," she said.

Zhongmei stood by the wall.

"Hold up your arms," the young woman said. She took out a yellow cloth tape measure, put one end of it on Zhongmei's shoulder, and measured the distance to the tips of her fingers. She wrote a number down in a notebook, and then measured the rest of Zhongmei's body, the distance from elbow to shoulder, wrist to elbow, waist to just under her neck, her hips to her knees, her knees to her ankles.

"That's pretty good," the girl said, writing down numbers. "OK, stand with your back against the wall."

Zhongmei did as she was told.

"Now rotate your hips. Keep facing front and try to touch the wall to the right with your right knee and then the wall on the left with your left knee."

Zhongmei did it easily.

"You're very flexible," the young woman said appreciatively. She asked Zhongmei to do a few more exercises. Zhongmei held her leg up so that the front of her shin touched her chin. She bent forward at the waist, keeping her legs straight, and was able to touch the floor with her elbows. The young woman held Zhongmei by the waist and told her to see how far she could bend backward. Zhongmei bent back so that the top of her head touched the floor.

"Very good," the young woman said. "You've made it to the next stage." She filled out a card, and wrote down a date and a time—the date was for the next day and the time was eight in the morning. "Show this at the entrance when you get here, and come back to studio eleven," she said.

"But what about my dance?" Zhongmei said.

"What dance?" the young woman asked.

"I've prepared a dance for the judges," Zhongmei said. "When do I get to do it?"

The girl laughed. "You may never get to do it," she said. "You have to get through the first stages of the audition before you dance."

"How many stages are there?" Zhongmei asked.

"Seven," the young woman said.

"Seven!" said Zhongmei.

"That's right, seven," the young woman said. "You've made it past the first one. You've got a long way to go."

A letter was waiting for Zhongmei when she got back to Policeman Li's house that night. It was addressed to Chen Aiyi's house on Old Stone Bridge Lane, but that address was crossed out and Policeman Li's written under it, no doubt by Chen Aiyi.

Dear Zhongmei,

We just got your letter and everybody is very worried about you. Ba can't understand why Policeman Li didn't pick you up at the train station. We all think you should come home. Use the rest of the money you have to buy a ticket, and send a telegram, so we will know when you will get here. Everybody is fine. We know you are staying with Huping's family, so you are safe. But we're worried and hope you will be home soon.

From Da-jie

Dear Da-jie, Zhongmei wrote back.

The mail is slow, and you didn't get my last letter yet, but when you do, you'll see that everything is fine. (Please write to me at Policeman Li's from now.) And I have good news. The audition started today, and I passed the first stage! I didn't do any dancing. They just measured my body and tested me for flexibility. The girl said I was very flexible. I got a card. You need a card to go to the next stage, and there are seven stages all together. I was very happy to get a card today, but who knows if I'll get one tomorrow. A lot of other girls were crying today because they didn't get cards. I'm going to keep mine in a very safe place.

Once again, Policeman Li's motorcycle rumbled up to the Dance Academy gate and Zhongmei hopped off. She went up the two flights of stairs to studio eleven, where a different young woman took more detailed measurements of Zhongmei's body. She spent a long time measuring distances and circumferences before nodding approvingly. "Your legs are sixteen inches longer than your torso," she told Zhongmei. "That's the best I've seen so far," she said as she handed Zhongmei a card to return the next day.

Zhongmei was ecstatic, though she didn't know why it was good to have legs longer than her torso, so she asked.

"It means you still have quite a lot to grow," the second young woman explained, "and it's good for dancers to be tall."

By the third day there were a lot fewer girls at the school, and Zhongmei realized it was because thousands of the candidates had already been eliminated. She was getting used to the scene in the courtyard outside, where family members awaited the girls at the end of the day. Some girls came out of the building holding up the precious card that gave them an appointment for the next level, and there would be cheers from the waiting family members. But many girls emerged through the door with tear-streaked cheeks and no cards, and there was no mistaking the stricken looks, the dashed hopes written on the faces of their family members. Zhongmei felt so bad for those without cards that by the end of the third day she hid hers under her arm when she went down the stairs so as not to make anybody feel jealous.

On the afternoon of the third day, a new set of testers

appeared, older than the first. They seemed to be the people in real authority at the Dance Academy, teachers and administrators. Each girl was asked a few questions by one of these older people.

"Why do you want to come to the Beijing Dance Academy?" a short round woman with gray hair asked Zhongmei.

"Because I love dance," Zhongmei said, feeling that it was a silly question with an all-too-obvious answer: because she would have a much more exciting life here than back home in Baoquanling, but she didn't say that.

"Have you performed before?"

"Oh, yes, I performed a lot in my hometown."

"It's a rather small place, your hometown. You really had chances to perform there?"

"Yes, lots of chances," Zhongmei said quite honestly. "I sang almost every day, and I danced a lot too with the Propaganda Brigade."

"Are you ready to work very hard?"

"Yes," Zhongmei said.

"I mean really hard, harder than most people will ever have to work in their lives," the woman said. "This school is not for fun. It's to train the best professional dancers in China, and I can tell you, it's going to hurt every day. Are you really ready for that?"

"I'm ready!" Zhongmei exclaimed.

"Are you sure? I can promise you it will be the hardest thing you'll ever do. You'll be so tired at the end of the day you almost won't be able to change into your pajamas and get into bed. And if you don't do well, you'll be sent home, and you'll never come back."

"I'm sure," Zhongmei said.

"OK," the woman said. "I'm going to pass you into the fourth stage. Come back tomorrow at eight o'clock and be prepared to perform a dance you know. Go to studio eight. Maybe there's something you did in Bao . . . what was it?"

"Baoquanling," Zhongmei reminded her.

"Yes, there," the woman said. "You'll need music. Do you have music?"

"No," said Zhongmei.

"You didn't come with sheet music?"

"No, I didn't know I was supposed to."

"Well, I guess they don't know much up there in Bao . . . whatever," the woman said. "You say you used to sing."

"Yes."

"Then be prepared to accompany yourself by singing. It's a little unusual, but maybe the judges will remember you better that way." The woman smiled. "Good luck," she said.

9

"Have I Done All This for Nothing?"

*O*n the next morning, there were hundreds of girls already forming a line in front of the Dance Academy entrance. It was a bit like the first day, though with fewer people. Parents and brothers and sisters nervously stood with their daughters and sisters under the row of locust trees on the street outside. As always, only Zhongmei was alone. She could see a long line of boys extending down the street on the opposite side of the gate. She waited and waited, rehearsing in her mind the dance she had practiced in Baoquanling from *The Red Detachment of Women*, a ballet about a girl chained in a dungeon by an evil landlord. She escapes and joins the revolutionary army led by Chairman Mao. Zhongmei had often sung one of the songs from the opera over the town loudspeaker—"Forward, forward under the banner of Mao Zedong; forward to victory"— and while the lyrics were pretty simple, she went over them again now, just to be sure that if she was seized with panic, she wouldn't forget them. While she hummed, she felt the dance movements inside her even though she didn't actually do them out there on the sidewalk.

"What's your name?" a girl next to her asked, interrupting her reverie. She was a little shorter and a little plumper than Zhongmei. She wore a black blouse printed with bright red butterflies that matched perfectly with a tailored red skirt. "I'm Wang Tianyuan."

"Li Zhongmei," Zhongmei said, and smiled, glad to have some company.

"I came from Shanghai with my grandmother," Tianyuan said. She nodded at a short, chubby woman wearing a well-tailored Mao suit standing nearby. You could always tell the people in China who were officials of the government. Their tailored blue or gray suits, in the style made popular by Chairman Mao, were made out of fine cotton or wool, compared to the rougher, baggier, store-bought cotton jackets and pants worn by ordinary people. The pants were pleated and loose-fitting. The matching jacket had a collar that buttoned at the neck.

"*Ni hao, xiao-mei*"—Hello, little miss—Tianyuan's grandmother said to Zhongmei.

"*Ni hao, ai-yi*," Zhongmei said back.

"Where are you from?" Tianyuan asked her.

"I'm from Baoquanling," Zhongmei replied, hesitating a bit because she knew that Tianyuan was unlikely to have heard of it.

"Where's that?" Tianyuan said.

"It's in Heilongjiang," Zhongmei said, and Tianyuan looked

as mystified as if Zhongmei had said she had come to the audition from Mars.

"You came all the way from Heilongjiang?" she said in what seemed like wonderment but was actually a kind of criticism, because she then proceeded to tell Zhongmei that she had no chance of being accepted at the Beijing Dance Academy so it was silly to have made such a big effort to come to it.

"Don't you know, they've already chosen all the students," she said. "The audition is just for show, to make it look like everybody has a chance, but really, all the decisions have already been made."

"Be quiet, Tianyuan," her grandmother said. "You shouldn't be telling people that."

But Zhongmei was already absorbing this shocking piece of information. She was also noticing Tianyuan's nice store-bought clothes and her pale soft skin, the skin of somebody who didn't have to brave the scorching summers and numbing winters of northern Heilongjiang. Zhongmei felt coarse and leathery compared to her.

"They've already chosen everybody?" Zhongmei said, amazed and not quite believing that it could be true. "But . . ."

"I know that because my mother's good friend is a teacher at the school, and she told me—my mother, I mean. That's why we came here instead of going to the audition in Shanghai, because my mother's friend is in Beijing."

"Hush, Tianyuan," the grandmother put in, but to no avail.

"You mean, you've been chosen?" Zhongmei asked, incredulous.

"Oh, yes," Tianyuan said. "You have to have *guanxi*." She used the term in China for "connections, friends in high places," and Zhongmei remembered her father's first reaction when she said she wanted to go to the auditions, that the Li family had no *guanxi*. And now here was another eleven-year-old girl saying the same thing: in order to get something really good, you had to know powerful people, and if you didn't know powerful people, you would never get those things.

"We have great *guanxi*," Tianyuan said proudly, "since my father is the head of the Shanghai Film School, and then there's my mother's friend who teaches here. She was once a famous ballerina. She studied with masters in Russia."

As the girls were talking, there was suddenly a stir in the crowd as a green sedan pulled up to the school entrance and a handsome man in a well-tailored Mao suit got out.

"It's him!" Zhongmei heard somebody say, as she was jostled by somebody behind her trying to get a better look. She watched as the man smiled at the people standing in line and then turned to walk into the school courtyard. He was the most elegant person Zhongmei had ever seen, tall, fine-featured, and clearly self-confident. But there was also something modest about him, a kind of embarrassment at attracting so much attention.

"Who's that?" Zhongmei asked Tianyuan.

"You don't know who that is?" Tianyuan said.

"Don't talk like that, Tianyuan," the girl's grandmother said. "Not everybody knows the dance world as well as you do."

"That's Jia Zuoguang," Tianyuan said.

Jia Zuoguang. The name rang a distant bell for Zhongmei. It was a name she had heard before, but she wasn't sure where or when.

"He's only the greatest dancer in China," Tianyuan said. "Now he's the vice director of the Beijing Dance Academy, but even though he's only the vice director, he's really the person in charge. He's the one who can have you accepted if he likes you. But I've already told you, if you don't have *guanxi*, you don't stand much of a chance."

Zhongmei remembered where she had heard the name Jia Zuoguang before. It had been during her week with the song and dance troupe of Jiamusi, when she had gone there with her teacher from Baoquanling. She remembered now that the members of the troupe had all watched a dance movie and Jia Zuoguang had been the lead male dancer in it. She remembered his strength as a dancer, the grace and height of his leaps. Somebody had said that he had even once been to Jiamusi when he had toured northern Heilongjiang Province a few years before.

"But he can't help you really," Tianyuan was saying. "There's already a list of names. My mother's friend has seen the list, and my name is on it. It's all the sons and daughters of important people like my father. No farmer's daughter from Heilongjiang is going to get on that list."

Zhongmei watched as Jia Zuoguang disappeared through the main gate of the school, gently pushing his way through the crowd.

"Is that all you need, *guanxi*?" Zhongmei said. She suddenly had a vision of important people who worked in offices and wore fine woolen tailored suits and were chauffeured around in big black Red Flag limousines. Once she had seen such a car in Baoquanling, as long as an ocean liner, carrying the governor of Heilongjiang Province in an inspection tour of the state farm. Of course these important people had children. Were they the ones already chosen?

"You mean you don't even have to be a good dancer?" Zhongmei asked. "You just have to have high-ranking parents?"

"Oh, no, you have to be a good dancer too. I'm already very famous in Shanghai. I was the best dancer in the Shanghai Children's Dance Troupe. Everybody knows me!"

"Well, I was famous too," Zhongmei said truthfully.

"But you have no *guanxi*, being from ... what was the name of that place again?"

"Baoquanling," Zhongmei reminded her.

"What dance are you going to do today?" Tianyuan asked.

"It's from *The Red Detachment of Women*," Zhongmei said. "What about you?"

"Oh, I'm doing a solo from *Swan Lake*," Tianyuan replied. "That's real ballet. *The Red Detachment of Women* was really a Gang of Four ballet," she said. "I don't think the judges are going to like it."

The Gang of Four were a group of high officials in China who were close to Chairman Mao. One of them, the leading one, was Mao's wife, Jiang Qing, who had created a few ballets and operas that for about ten years were just about all the

Chinese people were allowed to see or hear. The Gang of Four were the ones who had instigated a lot of the violence during the Cultural Revolution, and they were reviled for that all over China. A few months after Mao died, the new government arrested them, put them on trial, and sent them to jail. It's true what Tianyuan said, that *The Red Detachment of Women* had been one of Jiang Qing's favorites, and it was full of bombastic praise for Mao and the Communist Party. But even though Mao's wife was now in prison, it was still performed a lot, especially in the countryside. Foreign ballets like *Swan Lake* had been banned in China during the Gang of Four time, but they were making a comeback now, especially in the big cities.

"Well, it's what I prepared," Zhongmei said worriedly. "I don't have time to switch to something else."

"Do you have the music? Can I see it?" Tianyuan asked, as if that would somehow help.

"I don't have any music. I didn't bring any."

"You don't have music? But how are you planning to perform it, then?"

"I'm going to sing," Zhongmei said, her worries increasing.

"You're going to sing?" Tianyuan spoke with a kind of mirthful astonishment, the tone an adult might use on a child when the child says something very foolish but also cute.

"They said I could do that," Zhongmei replied. "Why not?"

"Well, I've never heard of it," Tianyuan said. "I have my sheet music." She showed Zhongmei a plastic folder she was carrying.

"Anyway," Tianyuan said, "it really wouldn't matter even

if you did have a score since what you don't have is *guanxi*. I guess you couldn't, coming from a place nobody's ever heard of like this Bao . . . what?"

"Baoquanling," Zhongmei said, feeling small and unworthy.

"Baoquanling," Tianyuan repeated. "They're only taking twelve girls and twelve boys from all the auditions all over the country, and there are a lot more than twelve boys and twelve girls who are good and have *guanxi*. I wouldn't get my hopes up if I were you."

A couple of hours later Zhongmei and Tianyuan split up, each going to a different studio for her prepared dance. Zhongmei went up to studio eight, where she found a few dozen girls sitting or standing in the corridor outside the door. Looking through the door's glass pane, she could see a panel of three judges sitting at a table at the back of the room. One girl ahead of her was still doing her performance, accompanied on the studio piano by a man Zhongmei hadn't seen up to that point. When the girl was finished, the head judge told her to wait in the corridor outside and signaled to Zhongmei to step forward.

"Name please?" he said.

"Li Zhongmei," Zhongmei said.

The man looked down at a ledger book in front of him and made a notation with his pen.

"If you have sheet music for the accompanist, you may give it to him now," the judge said.

"I'm going to accompany myself by singing," Zhongmei announced.

"You're going to sing?" The man sounded a bit incredulous.

"Yes," Zhongmei said.

The man shrugged. "All right. Proceed."

Zhongmei took her place in the middle of the studio, wearing her special yellow dress with the brown straps and her green shoes. She did her dance and sang, her clear, flutey voice, so familiar to the farmers of Baoquanling, bouncing off the walls of the studio as she enacted the drama of the girl fighting against the men of the evil landlord. Her dance was very acrobatic, involving numerous high leg kicks and leaps, but despite the exertion, her voice never faltered.

"Please wait outside with the others," the head judge told her when she was finished.

Zhongmei, flushed from her effort, found a spot to sit down along the wall of the corridor, already crowded with girls, and watched as more candidates were summoned into the studio, each of them emerging, their faces red, their upper lips beaded with sweat, back into the corridor a few minutes later. After a long time, the head judge appeared at the studio door with a piece of paper in his hand.

"When I read your name," he said, "please come up and take your card for tomorrow. If you don't hear your name, that means you are dismissed, with our thanks for coming to the audition and our best wishes for your future."

The man started reading the names off his list, and with each name there was a scream of happiness and a girl running up to him and taking her card. Zhongmei counted the number of names—five, six, seven, then eleven, twelve, thirteen, but not hers, not yet. Her heart began to pound as the man read off the list. Until that moment, she had continued to think that she wouldn't make it, and that each day of the audition merely extended what had become the main purpose of her visit, which was to see a bit of Beijing, to glimpse the big world outside her hometown, before she returned there for good. Yet, at the same time, she dreamed that she would be accepted, but since she knew she wouldn't be, she had steeled herself against too much disappointment when the day on which she failed to get a card finally came.

Now, however, her hope had become independent of her rational will. It was like a little animal gripping her chest from inside, making it hard even to breathe. "Please," she said to herself, "give me just one more day. Please don't bring this to an end now." She thought of the girl she'd met outside and her claim that the whole thing was a sham, and she felt a mixture of anger and disbelief rise up inside her. It can't be true what she said, she thought, even as she worried that maybe it was true. The girl had seemed awfully sure of herself, and her grandmother, dressed in that sleek wool suit, didn't contradict her. She just told her not to talk about it. Well, if it was true, Zhongmei then thought, it would be no disgrace to be rejected at the audition, since it wouldn't be her talent that was being judged, but her nonexistent *guanxi*. And yet, could it really be that the selections had already secretly been made? Could something so sneaky and deceitful take place in China?

"Li Zhongmei." Zhongmei was so intent on these thoughts that she didn't hear her name at first.

"Li Zhongmei" was pronounced again, and Zhongmei realized with a start that she was being called to pick up her card for the next day! Suddenly, like the girls before her, she screamed. She leaped up off the corridor floor and ran for her card, as if it might be withdrawn if she didn't grab it right away. She was so out of breath that she had to gasp for air after her scream, and she realized she had hardly been breathing from the time the head judge had started reading the list.

Zhongmei rushed into Policeman Li's house that night happy and excited. "I made it to the next stage!" she told Da-ma, who smiled broadly and clapped her hands. Adding to her excitement was a letter from Zhongqin.

> Dear Zhongmei,
>   Everybody's really glad you finally found
> Policeman Li. Ma and Ba are fine. One of the
> hens hatched some eggs and the courtyard is
> full of little yellow chicks chirping all day. Your
> *da-ge* and your *xiao-di* and your *er-jie* are all fine.
> It's getting cold here. Ma is making a quilted
> jacket for you for winter and she'll send it to you.
> Everybody wishes you luck at the audition. Try
> your best. You can't do more than that, but you
> have to be sure that it is your best. It's your one
> chance. It's no shame if you don't make it,
> but it would be a shame if you don't give it all
> you've got.
>   Zhongqin

Dear Da-jie,

I've got good news. I did my dance from *The Red Detachment of Women* today, and guess what? I've made it to the fifth stage! So there's no question I'm giving it all I've got. A girl I met told me it was a mistake to choose *Red Detachment* because it was a Gang of Four production, but I guess it didn't matter. The girl was from Shanghai. She danced something from *Swan Lake*. That's a famous foreign ballet. I didn't see her perform. She told me I'm wasting my time, since all the girls who are going to get in have already been selected in secret. I asked Policeman Li about what she said, and he said it was nonsense, but then he shook his head in a way that made me feel he was only trying to make me feel better. Do you think it could be true? Have I done all this for nothing?

Your little sister

After she finished writing her letter, Zhongmei ate a bowl of Da-ma's sweet red bean soup. She helped with the dishes, washing them in an enamel basin in the small courtyard of their house, spilling the dirty dishwater over the brick floor. Then she and Policeman Li sat on folding stools in the lane outside their house, enjoying the cool weather. There wasn't much to do in Beijing at night in those years, before everybody had televisions and computers or the money to go out to restaurants and the movies, like they do today. The houses were built behind high brick walls and, except for their entranceways, couldn't be seen from the street. But in the nice weather, everybody put little wooden chairs outside their front doorways and said hello to each other. Policeman Li smoked. Zhongmei listened to the twangy sound of an *er-hu* being played by an invisible person behind one of the lane's walls, and Zhongmei asked Policeman Li if he knew who it was.

"Oh, that's Old Blind Ma," Policeman Li said.

"He's blind?" Zhongmei said.

"Can't see a thing. He lives two houses down and across the lane. He gives people massages during the day. Did you know that that's what a lot of blind people do?"

Zhongmei had vaguely heard that.

"You do what you can," Policeman Li said, and sighed. "Instead of feeling sorry for yourself, you do your best to be useful, right?"

"Yes," Zhongmei agreed. She thought about how Zhongqin had given her similar advice in her letter. You do your best. You can't do any more, but be sure that it is your best.

A short time later she and Policeman Li went inside to go to bed. People turned in very early in China then, even in big cities like Beijing. By nine o'clock the streets were pretty much deserted and a silence that reminded Zhongmei of Baoquanling settled over the city. Except on this night, the *er-hu* player continued to play, so that Zhongmei drifted off to sleep with Old Blind Ma's melody pleasantly in her head, mingling with a new thought: she had made it this far. There were three stages to go. For the first time Zhongmei began ardently to want to succeed,

102

no matter what Wang Tianyuan might have told her about her having no chance. This was no longer just a sort of excuse for an adventure, a chance to have her picture taken outside the Forbidden City while she pursued what she had come to accept was an impossible dream. Now she was determined to do everything she could to make the dream entirely possible.

On the fifth day, Zhongmei went again to studio eight, where she found a crowd of other girls and a panel of three judges sitting at a table. A woman collected all the candidates' cards at the entrance.

"My name is Liu Lingzhang," she said, "and I'll be your instructor for stage five of the audition. I'm going to teach you a few dance sequences and then each of you will perform them in turn in front of the judges." She turned toward the panel of two women and a man.

Zhongmei watched the movements of the sequence carefully. She was nervous when it was her turn to perform them, but she was determined to do them all without a mistake, and she did. At the end of the day, once again she got the coveted card instructing her to return. It told her to report to the school's main auditorium at the usual time, eight o'clock in the morning. Again, she and a few other girls skipped happily to the courtyard while most of the others trudged sadly down the stairs, knowing that they would never be coming back.

The auditorium was a large room on the first floor of the academy, and when Zhongmei arrived there the next morning, she saw a long table set up at the head of the room directly under the portrait of Chairman Mao, and dozens of girls and boys milling about, the lucky few who were still in contention. Zhongmei tried to count the number of them, and she got up to sixty with quite a few left uncounted when a hush settled over the room and the judges, appearing from a side entrance, took their places at the table.

"Good morning," one of them said. He was the tall, elegant, and handsome man that Zhongmei instantly recognized as the very Jia Zuoguang whom she had seen getting out of his car outside the school two days before, the greatest dancer in China!

"I want to congratulate all of you for getting to stage six of the 1978 audition for the Beijing Dance Academy, the first truly open audition the school has ever had," he said. "That's already a great achievement and you should all be proud. Every one of you has already shown that you have what it takes to be a dancer. But as you know, there are spots for only twelve boys and twelve girls in the class that will come to school at the end of August, and we are going to choose just seven boys and seven girls from the audition here in Beijing. There are still more than one hundred of you in the room today, one hundred and twenty to be exact, and that's one hundred and twenty out of more than twenty thousand candidates who began this audition a week ago. That means that all of you have already done very well."

Zhongmei's heart fluttered as she listened. The greatest dancer in China, and he was there right in front of her in the very same room! Zhongmei had never seen anybody famous before in person. But Jia Zuoguang seemed not only famous to her. There was a calm gentleness about him. He didn't have the bluster and self-importance of so many officials in China. He seemed nice.

"One more thing," Jia continued. "Of course you should all try hard in the last two stages of the audition, but don't be too disappointed if you aren't one of the lucky fourteen. Of course I know that you will be disappointed, but I hope not so much that you'll be discouraged from continuing to dance. You're all good, and there are other schools in China for dance, other opportunities for you, and I'm sure you will all find them."

Don't be disappointed? Other schools? Zhongmei heard those words, but to her they meant the exact opposite of what Jia intended them to mean. Seeing Jia made her feel that there was nothing else in the world that mattered other than being selected for the Beijing Dance Academy. There was no other school in the world for her but this one. There was no other place for her than right here where he was.

"Today," Jia was saying, "the procedure will change. Yesterday you went in a small group to a studio to perform some sequences that were taught to you. That part will not change. Some teachers will introduce you to a series of steps, and you will perform them, not in a small studio but right here in front of the main panel.

"After that," Jia continued, "the judges will meet to decide a list of fifty finalists—twenty-five girls and twenty-five boys— who will be invited back for stage seven of the audition. So as not to require that you wait here while our meeting takes

105

place, instead of giving you cards at the end of the day, we will post the names in the display case in front of the school, and starting at eight o'clock tomorrow morning, you will be able to come to see if your name is on the list. The final stage of the audition will start the day after tomorrow at the same time, eight o'clock."

Jia then waved at a teacher who emerged into the middle of the room to show the candidates the steps they would have to perform. The first ones were pretty easy, and Zhongmei, when her turn came, did them with no problem. They got harder as the day wore on, and Zhongmei watched as some of the candidates stumbled, and a few of them even fell. But she didn't fail to notice that some of the girls were very good. Before Zhongmei was called for the final sequence of steps, she heard the name Wang Tianyuan called, and she watched the girl who was sure she had already been chosen do her steps. She looked good, Zhongmei felt. She was a good dancer, strong and sure, but Zhongmei also noted that she seemed a little short and slightly pudgy, not sleek and long-limbed like most of the other girls. Also, at the very end of her dance, during a movement that wound up with the dancer standing on one leg, the other raised behind her, her arms spread like a bird in flight, Zhongmei saw a bit of wobble, and that gave her some hope. If she could do that movement without wobbling, Zhongmei thought, then it would mean that she was better than Tianyuan and that would mean, *guanxi* or not, that she should be chosen ahead of her. It would be nice, Zhongmei thought, if both of them got into the school; if only one of them could make it, it should be the one who was better.

Zhongmei didn't wobble. And when the day finished, she felt that she had done well. But so had a lot of other girls, and anyway, maybe, as Tianyuan had told her, the whole audition was a sham.

And so, naturally, she was in a state of high excitement when she arrived the next morning at eight o'clock sharp on Policeman Li's motorcycle. Zhongmei bolted to the display case before they had come to a full stop. Two sheets of paper each with two rows of names were posted, and there was already a good deal of pushing and shoving as girls and their parents tried to get close enough to read it. Alongside was another display case, in front of which boys and their parents were doing the same thing.

In Chinese, there is no alphabetical order, because there are no letters in Chinese like there are in languages like English, French, and Spanish. Instead, words are formed by what are called Chinese characters, each character representing a sort of picture of its meaning. Each last name is indicated by a single character, and characters are organized by the number of strokes it takes to form that character.

When Zhongmei got near enough to the fateful piece of paper to read it, she quickly scanned down the list. Along the way she saw Wang Tianyuan. Wang has four strokes, so it is higher in the order of characters than Li, which requires six strokes. Despite her wobble the day before, she had made it to the final stage, which made Zhongmei think that maybe she was right, maybe the decision about who would be accepted had already been made, and that would be bad for Zhongmei, because she knew that no arrangement existed for her to get into the school. But she didn't think about that for long. She scanned rapidly down the list to the surname Li. There were five of them, Li being a very common name, and Zhongmei frantically devoured the full names of each of them—Li Xiaohua, Li Zhaoping, Li Xuenian, Li Linghao, and then, there it was—Li Zhongmei, written in clear, squarish characters. She had been chosen for stage seven!

10

"I'm Not Going Back Until I Dance!"

The next morning, Zhongmei found herself wishing that Policeman Li would drive faster. She sat on the back of his motorcycle, the wind ruffling her hair, hardly noticing as they negotiated the narrow lanes near Li Zhongshan's old house, rolled down some broader avenues lined with gray cement-block apartment houses, and roared past a walled park and another neighborhood of narrow twisting lanes before pulling up to the Beijing Dance Academy.

Stage seven would be held in a large studio on the second floor. Once again, Vice Director Jia greeted the candidates and made a short speech.

"In the final stage of the audition," he said, "we will ask every candidate, both boys and girls, to do an improvisation. Each candidate will pick a piece of paper out of a bowl. The word on the paper will be your theme. You will read it aloud, and then, right away, with no time for preparation, you will make up a three- to five-minute dance expressing that theme.

You will be something from nature—a bird, a rabbit, the wind, a cloud, a peony, a rose, a tiger, a mouse, or something else.

"You will take a piece of paper out of the bowl when it's your turn," Jia said, and Zhongmei noticed something new in his tone, something stricter, just a bit harder than before. There were no words of encouragement for those who wouldn't be selected, like there had been the day before.

"There will be a piano accompanist," he said. "And this is very important: you must begin right away, as soon as the music starts. Once you have performed, you may return home. A list of the boys and girls chosen to attend the Dance Academy will be posted, like yesterday morning, on a sheet of paper in the display case."

Jia told all the candidates to leave the auditorium and to wait in the courtyard until their names were called, and so everybody filed out of the building nervously to wait their turn. The atmosphere, always tense, was especially so now. Nobody spoke. Zhongmei saw Tianyuan standing with her grandmother, and she saw that Tianyuan saw her, but they didn't say anything to each other. There were fifty eleven-year-olds there, and it made Zhongmei a little sad to think that all but seven of the girls and seven of the boys were going to be sent home. To have made it as far as stage seven and then in the end to be told that you had not been chosen seemed almost cruel to her.

Finally Zhongmei heard her name called, and she entered the large room where the improvisations were taking place. She watched as the girl just in front of her finished her turn, and then Zhongmei stepped forward and faced the table of judges. She managed a smile, but she had never been so scared in her life.

A large blue porcelain bowl materialized in front of her, held by one of the girls who had measured her body in what now seemed like an event from a long time ago. Zhongmei took a piece of paper, unfolded it, and gulped when she saw the word on it.

"*Tsao*," she said, looking at Vice Director Jia—grass. He didn't smile. His previous gentleness had disappeared. He was now an official carrying out his duty, and Zhongmei, expecting a friendlier tone, was disconcerted. Instantly the accompanist started in on the piano. Zhongmei listened for just a bar or so before starting her improvisation. Grass, she thought. She had expected an animal, perhaps a flower, but grass? She remembered later that she was struck by the beauty of the music, and maybe she was waiting also for some sign of encouragement from Jia, and these two things and her puzzlement about grass were the reasons for her delay. But it was only a short one. She took her initial pose, and moved to take her first step when, at a signal from Jia, the accompanist stopped, and she was left on the floor in front of the judges frozen in place, not knowing what to do.

"Next!" Jia said.

Zhongmei stood in stunned silence.

"Thank you," the school's vice director said. "You may step to the side."

Zhongmei didn't move. "What?" she said.

"Step aside," Jia said, looking past Zhongmei. "Next candidate, please," he said, and the girl who had been just behind Zhongmei in the line stepped alongside her.

"But I haven't done my improvisation!" Zhongmei said.

"We waited for you, and you didn't dance," Jia told her. His voice was impatient. The nice man of a few days before seemed to have vanished.

"But," Zhongmei stammered.

"Please move over for the next girl."

"But I didn't have my chance yet!" Zhongmei protested. "I want to do my dance!"

"You were given your chance, and you didn't take it and that's that," came Jia's no-nonsense voice. "Next candidate!"

Zhongmei didn't leave.

"You're holding up the line," Jia said. "We don't have time for anybody to perform twice."

"But I didn't perform even once," Zhongmei insisted.

"I said very clearly at the beginning that you must begin your dance right away. You didn't. So please step aside," Jia commanded. He leaned forward and glared at Zhongmei, who shuddered at the force of his authority. Resigned, she took a step or two backward to leave the room, which seemed to be spinning slowly around her, the walls rotating on some invisible axis, the portrait of Chairman Mao, the table of judges, Jia himself, drifting to the right.

Zhongmei closed her eyes for a second to try to get the room to stay still, and as she did so, standing there in the momentary darkness, she made a decision that changed her whole life. For no doubt, if she had obediently turned to the auditorium's exit and walked away as ordered, she would have lost her chance to be a student at the Beijing Dance Academy forever, and the dream that had been taking shape in her mind as she passed each stage of the audition would have come to nothing. But standing there with her eyes closed in the rotating room, she heard a small voice inside her telling her, "No! You got this far. Don't just meekly retreat like a wounded dog. Put up a fight. Be like that girl in *The Red Detachment of Women* who stood up to the evil landlord and his henchmen!"

"I'm not leaving until I do my improvisation!" Zhongmei said, her words defiant but a quavering in her voice betraying her fear.

She could hear the gasps of astonished disapproval of the people around her. She knew that what she was doing amounted to an extraordinary act of disobedience for any eleven-year-old girl, but it was especially extraordinary in China, where disobedience tended to be treated very harshly.

As Zhongmei stood there, she saw Jia nod toward a man and a woman at the side of the room, their red armbands emblazoned with the word *anquan*, security in Chinese. The two guards stirred and walked across the floor toward Zhongmei, with the clear intention of dragging her out of the room and putting her on the next train to Baoquanling. Zhongmei watched them approach out of the corner of her eye. She noted the scowls of disapproval on their faces. She heard the stunned silence in the room. She felt the angry, astonished eyes of the judges upon her. She had never felt as completely alone as she felt at that moment.

"I traveled for three days and two nights to get here!"

she yelled suddenly, desperate for some understanding of her predicament, the loudness of her voice surprising even her. "My mother and father had to borrow money for the train ticket," she said, lowering the volume just a bit, then raising it again, "and I'm not going back until I dance!"

"I told you, no repeat performances, young lady," Jia said.

Now the man and the woman were standing next to Zhongmei, one on each side of her, waiting for further instructions on what to do with this disobedient girl. Zhongmei felt the strong hand of the woman grip her upper arm and start to pull her to the side.

"It's not my fault that the accompanist started playing so quickly," Zhongmei said, pulling back. "He didn't give me a chance."

There's no doubt that Zhongmei would have lost this battle and been taken away ignominiously, but Jia detected something about her. Perhaps it was something in her country accent, or in her story about having spent three days traveling to the audition, or maybe he was touched by her homemade and somewhat overdone costume, the yellow skirt and the pink blouse and the two rows of embroidered ducks, so quaintly different from the fashionable store-bought clothes of the other girls. Or possibly it was simply the audacity of her refusal to go away obediently and never see the inside of the Beijing Dance Academy again. Zhongmei saw him signal to the security guards to wait, and she felt the grip on her shoulder loosen.

"Where did you come from that's so far it took you three days and two nights to get here?" he asked, and Zhongmei heard a faint softening of his tone, a little bit of the kindness she had detected before.

"It's a very small place; nobody here's heard of it," she said.

In fact, as a little girl, Zhongmei always believed Baoquanling to be a rather big place, as it was a lot bigger than her and bigger than a lot of surrounding villages. Its paved main streets, lined with state-run shops and state farm administrative offices, seemed very wide to her, the distance from home to her school seemed far, and so did the wheat fields and pigpens where her parents went to work every day before dawn. It was only after Zhongmei had seen Harbin and gotten to Beijing and people like Tianyuan asked her where she was from that she realized Baoquanling was a very small place and that nobody had heard of it.

"Well, where is it?" Jia asked.

"It's in Heilongjiang," Zhongmei said. She knew that Vice Director Jia would at least have heard of her province, which was itself bigger than most medium-sized countries in the world.

"Where in Heilongjiang?" Jia asked.

"Jiamusi District."

"Where in Jiamusi District?"

"Luobei County," Zhongmei said.

"Where in Luobei County?"

"It's a very small place," Zhongmei said. "You've never heard of it."

"Where in Luobei County?" Jia repeated.

"It's called Baoquanling," Zhongmei said. "It's very small and you've never—"

"Baoquanling?" Jia said. Amazingly, with the word *Bao-*

quanling his whole countenance brightened. Suddenly he seemed very pleased. "You come from Baoquanling?"

"Yes," Zhongmei said, gladdened by this change in tone but mystified as to its meaning.

"Baoquanling on the Heilong River?"

"Yes," Zhongmei said.

"Right up there on the border with the Soviet Union?"

"Yes," Zhongmei said. "It's a state farm," she said, and repeated a few words of history that were drummed into every child at the Baoquanling Elementary School. "My father was in the army, and after he was demobilized, he and my mother followed the call of Chairman Mao to build socialism in China's unsettled border areas. We can see the Soviet Union from our side of the river."

"I've been there!" Jia said, his earlier formal, distant mood changing to one of delighted surprise. "I performed there once!"

"Really!" said Zhongmei happily. She remembered being told in Jiamusi that the greatest dancer in China had once toured the region.

"You came all the way from Baoquanling?" Jia said. He turned to the other members of the jury, who were seated at the table to the left and right of him. "It's a big state farm," he said for their benefit. "It's very impressive, built up by former army men from nothing." Turning to Zhongmei, he asked, "How did you get here?"

Zhongmei told him that she took the bus to Hegang and then another bus to Jiamusi and then the train to Harbin, and then another train . . .

李忠梅

11

Becoming Grass

"It's true that she has come a very long way," Jia interrupted. He turned to a woman, thin and angular, with yellowing plastic glasses, sitting next to him, and the two of them whispered to each other for what seemed to Zhongmei like a very long time. First Jia spoke into the ear of the woman, who frowned with obvious displeasure as she listened. Then she whispered into Jia's ear, waving her hand in the air as she did so, and when Jia whispered back, she looked aside with what seemed like an annoyed look on her face. Evidently the audition director's ruling was not what she wanted.

"You may perform," Vice Director Jia said, his voice taking on an official tone once again, "but you must start right away this time. If you don't, there will be no third chance. Your theme is grass. Proceed."

Needless to say, Zhongmei was very nervous, and for just the briefest of seconds, as she heard the accompanist start to play, she was gripped by a terrible fear. She felt everybody watching her, including the thin woman with the yellowing plastic glasses who had seemed to disagree with the decision to give her another chance. But knowing that she had to begin right away, before the first bar of the music had been played, she stepped toward the center of the room and raised her hands and swayed her body in what she supposed might be an approximation of grass. But she felt clumsy. Her legs, actually long and thin, seemed suddenly heavy and short. Her mind raced as she swayed a bit more and moved in a little circle, not because she had an idea for her improvisation but just to do something, anything, even as she knew that her raised arms and swaying body were neither very original nor very beautiful, just kind of obvious.

But while she moved, she listened to the music, finding it once again beautiful, and it was the music and her concentration on it that enabled her to enter a different sphere. All of a sudden she felt that she was entirely alone, not in a Beijing performance space being watched by the unsmiling and slightly bored faces of a half dozen judges sitting at a table in front of her, but by herself in a field. Yes, a field in the village of Precious Water from the Mountain Peaks in the province of Black Dragon River, which formed the remote northernmost part of China. She blotted out the thin woman and the room itself with its stained walls, hanging fluorescent lights, and picture of Chairman Mao. Jia himself slipped from her consciousness along with everything else—her thoughts and anxieties, her hopes and dreams of being one of the girls who would actually be chosen evaporated from her consciousness.

What occupied her mind's eye instead was just one thing, her transformation from a girl with a weight of worries on her thin shoulders into a single blade of grass, which was a deep, glorious, translucent emerald green. Quickly, as the music stole into her mind, Zhongmei studied this blade of grass, which took on a beautiful shape, thinner at the top than at the bottom, like a small, curved, delicate dagger. It stood under the springtime sun so that it was brilliantly illuminated on its upper side and in shadow on the other. She saw that drops of dew clung to its inner, shade-darkened edge, that it leaned over gracefully as if it were peering at something crawling nearby until a breeze sprang up and the blade stood upright, quivering for a second, and then swiftly leaned to the other side. It was a lithe, supple, slender extract of nature, and it had a story to tell, the story that Zhongmei, whose arms were raised and whose slender upper body leaned to one side, shook slightly, then hurled itself to the other side as if propelled by a sudden wind, began to express in dance. It was a story of birth, near death, and survival, of being made strong by the sun, growing tall, but then weakened by the wind, pelted by the rain, frozen by hail, and trampled under the muddy boots of men before springing back bruised but undefeated.

The blade of grass was like the servant girl in *The Red Detachment of Women*. She stood up to the injustices of man; the blade of grass endured the afflictions of both nature and man. Both were downtrodden. Both triumphed over adversity. Or, anyway, that's how Zhongmei, feeling the power of the story of a single blade of grass, sensing its possibilities, unaware of the eyes upon her, unconcerned, temporarily, with what was at stake, incarnated the heroic spirit of a single blade of grass, which moved her. She felt its fright and its resolve and its fragile strength and she fashioned those things into a story, which ended with the blade of grass bruised but triumphant.

She finished. The music stopped. Zhongmei emerged from her trance. The room, the table of judges, the Mao portrait, the security guards and other people standing along the walls, all of it having temporarily vanished, flickered back into existence. Zhongmei, flushed and breathing hard, bowed in the direction of the table, turned, and walked into the bright light of the courtyard outside.

She waited until six o'clock, watching the other girls as they emerged from their improvisations. She went home on Li Zhongshan's motorcycle as always. She heard the *er-hu* playing in her lane, and that soothed her jangling nerves, but she nonetheless slept fitfully, knowing that the announcement of the winning candidates would be made in the morning, on the usual piece of paper on the bulletin board.

She was up before dawn. Da-ma served her a breakfast of rice porridge, roasted peanuts, and pickled cabbage, but she was too excited to eat. She roared off on Li Zhongshan's motorcycle to the school.

"Try not to be disappointed," he told her on the way. "There were so many girls and they're only taking—"

"Yes, I know, and they're only taking seven," Zhongmei interrupted. "I won't be disappointed." But of course she knew that she was going to be crushed if her name was not on the list.

When they arrived at the Dance Academy building, she again sprang off the motorcycle before it had completely stopped and ran to the display case. Her eye was drawn to a single piece of paper where, inscribed in small, official-looking Chinese characters, was the news that transformed her life. "List of female candidates selected for attendance at the Beijing Dance Academy for the entering class of 1978," it said in formal red Chinese characters at the top of the sheet. Below were seven names, each of them three Chinese characters. It didn't take long to read them, and Zhongmei saw, with something like ecstatic stupefaction, that the characters *Li*, *Zhong*, and *Mei* were there. She was in!

Or could it be a mistake? She looked at each of the characters to be sure she wasn't hallucinating. *Li*, her family name, a long skinny character like this 李忠梅; then there was *Zhong*, and then *Mei*. She was not dreaming! There was no mistake! That was her name! She leaped into the air and screamed so that Li Zhongshan looked over, alarmed that something terrible had happened to her.

"They took me!" Zhongmei shouted, blissfully unconscious of the girls and boys who, having come so close, had not found their names on the list and were walking away dejectedly. She jumped up and down, both hands thrown above her head, not a blade of grass but a girl, triumphant. "My name is here!"

It was only sometime later when she was back at Policeman Li's house that she remembered the sad faces of those who had turned mournfully away even as Zhongmei expressed her happiness. One of the sad faces, she suddenly realized, had been that of Wang Tianyuan, with her grandmother looking

121

shocked and grim alongside her. The girl who had been so sure of herself hadn't been chosen after all. Zhongmei felt sorry. She didn't want her happiness to come at the cost of somebody else's happiness. Later, when she lay in her bed at Policeman Li's house, trying to get to sleep, she remembered something else that in her excitement she had been too busy to notice at the time. Zhongmei summoned up the scene at the display case in her mind's eye, and she shuddered when she realized that Tianyuan hadn't just been sad, but that she had also been looking at Zhongmei with hatred in her eyes.

Da-jie,

I'm in! It's unbelievable, but I made it! I mean, I'm one of the seven girls they've chosen. I'm so happy, and I'm scared stiff. Now I'll have to stay in Beijing, and you will be so far away. I have to do it, of course. But how will I manage?

Zhongmei

李忠梅

12
Comrade Tsang

Dear Zhongmei,

　　The whole of Baoquanling is celebrating
your success. No, it's bigger than Baoquanling.
It's all of Luobei County. Yesterday the county
party secretary came to our house in a big car
to congratulate Ma and Ba. The mayor of
Baoquanling came too. The whole lane turned
out to watch. And this morning there was a
picture of him and all of us in the newspaper.
You're very famous. It's just about the biggest
thing to happen here ever. Do well, work hard,
and don't forget us back home!

Zhongqin

Dear Da-jie,

　　How can you even think that I would ever
forget you? At the moment I'm terribly homesick.

I miss everybody, Er-jie, Da-ge, Xiao-di, and
especially you, Big Sister. If it hadn't been for
you, I would never have been able to come here.
You are my best friend, forever.

Zhongmei

Zhongmei had only gotten a one-way ticket when she
came to Beijing, and she didn't have enough money to go back
to Baoquanling for the rest of the summer, so she stayed at the
home of Policeman Li, his wife, and their son, Li Guang, for
the two months left before the term would begin at the Beijing
Dance Academy. It was true what she said about being homesick. She did miss her family. But it was also exciting to have
a few weeks in China's capital, and she used it to visit all the
famous places there. Usually she went with Li Guang. He took
lots of pictures of her, mostly dressed in her yellow pleated skirt
and pink blouse. There she was posing in front of the Forbidden City, the picture of Chairman Mao and the upturned eaves
of the imperial halls in the background. There were pictures of
her in front of the Temple of Heaven, whose luminous beauty
and grandeur left Zhongmei speechless. Li Guang took pictures
of her in front of the Confucius Temple and the Lama Temple.
She went to the Summer Palace and posed on the prow of the
famous marble barge, whose story she had learned at school.
It had been the pet project of a long-ago empress of China,
named Cixi, who diverted government money intended for
a real navy to build this beautiful but useless thing instead.
Zhongmei took long walks along the lake in Beihai Park,

where she and Li Guang went out in a rowboat. She learned about Beijing, which had been China's capital for most of the years since the Ming Dynasty six hundred years before!

She climbed Coal Hill behind the Forbidden City and got a view of the whole vast, incredible complex, which was testimony to the glories of China's past. The palace grounds stretched out in an immense rectangle surrounded by a high rust-red wall and moat. Ornate guard towers with curved, multilayered red-tile roofs stood at each corner of the complex and within was a splendid network of grand halls and smaller mansions, too many to count. It was magical, a fairy tale come true. Zhongmei had never even imagined anything at once so mighty and beautiful, and she was filled with pride in her country, realizing how great an honor it was to be called to the capital to study at one of its most famous institutions. To be sure, Baoquanling was nothing like this!

Finally the day came for Zhongmei to arrive at the Beijing Dance Academy. It was a crisp, sunny day at the end of August 1978 and, needless to say, Zhongmei was full of happy anticipation as she rode on the back of Policeman Li's motorcycle on what was now the familiar route to the school. Still, she stopped for a moment at the gate and read the brass plaque identifying the Beijing Wu-dao Xue-yuan, the Beijing Dance Academy, as if to confirm to herself that, yes, she was really going to be a member of that august institution. Just inside the gate was a small brick guardhouse, and Zhongmei saw an elderly man with a wispy white beard, wearing a

125

rumpled blue Mao suit, standing at the entrance and smiling at her.

"Are you one of the new students?" he said.

"Yes," said Zhongmei.

"Welcome," the man said. "My name is Zhou and I'm the night watchman. Everybody calls me Lao Ye, so you can too." As we've seen, *Lao ye* means "grandpa" in Chinese.

"And I'm Little Zhou," a girl a few years older than Zhongmei said. "No relation to Old Zhou, I mean, Lao Ye, I'm afraid." Little Zhou said she was a sixth-year student and was there to help the new girls get settled. She led Zhongmei to the dormitory building, which was diagonally across from the main classroom building where the auditions had taken place. "That's the cafeteria over there," she said, pointing to a two-story whitewashed building nearby. "And that's the theater on the other side of the cafeteria. That's where we have our special shows and competitions."

The dormitory was a low-ceilinged building with long dark corridors. Little Zhou led Zhongmei up a flight of stairs to the second floor. Zhongmei noticed a sign at the entrance to the corridor—NO BOYS ALLOWED. Little Zhou told her that all the first-year girls would share two dormitory rooms. Six girls, Zhongmei included, would be in the first room on the left, marked number one, and Zhongmei took it in at a glance. It had three double-decker bunk beds pressed against the walls, and between them were small metal desks and chests of drawers. Zhongmei had her small suitcase in her hand. It didn't contain all that much because Zhongmei didn't have all that much: a blouse, one pair of blue trousers, one padded suit for winter, two pairs of socks, two pairs of underwear, and a pair of cotton shoes, all made by her mother. She had a toothbrush and a plastic comb and the yellow skirt, pink blouse, and green shoes from Zhongqin and Zhongling. It only took a couple of minutes for her to put all of her possessions into the single drawer that Little Zhou said was hers. It was less than half full. She slid her suitcase under the lower berth of the bunk bed that Little Zhou said had been assigned to her.

"You'll sleep in this one," she said, patting the upper bunk.

Then, having done all she could for the moment, Zhongmei went back downstairs to survey the scene at the entrance. There was a great milling about. Cars pulled up to the front gate and disgorged boys and girls and their families, who carried suitcases through the courtyard and into the dormitory entrance. Zhongmei immediately noticed that most of the girls had larger suitcases than she did, or, in some cases, two suitcases, both larger than her single one. As usual she was the only arrival unaccompanied by a parent or two, a brother or a sister, some grandparents, sometimes entire three-generation families. Despite her excitement, she felt a stab of loneliness, but then she comforted herself with the thought that she too had a family, with four brothers and sisters. These other students didn't have anything that she didn't have. It's just that they had these things closer at hand. At the same time, Baoquanling, which Zhongmei had left three months earlier, seemed so far away it might as well have been on another planet.

Zhongmei went back upstairs and sat on her bed as her

classmates stuffed their clothes into the drawers assigned to them, using up a lot more of the drawer than Zhongmei had. Just when everybody was installed, there was a sudden banging noise as the door flew open and a large woman wearing a regulation gray Mao suit strode into the room, which suddenly went quiet.

"My name is Tsang," she said, "and I am the administrator of the Beijing Dance Academy. You will call me Tsang Tungzhi"—Comrade Tsang. "Listen carefully. I'm only going to say this once. These are the rules that you will strictly obey. Some of them are the rules of the Ministry of Culture and the school; some of them are my rules. But you must obey all of them, and you will be punished if you don't."

The seams of Comrade Tsang's suit seemed to strain against her stoutness, which gave her a look of great strength. Her voice seemed somehow to be amplified, as if she were speaking through a loudspeaker, though no loudspeaker was present. She had a broad, flat face with puffy eyes and closely cropped hair flecked with gray.

"First," Comrade Tsang resumed, "no one is allowed to have any money. You will hand over all of the money your parents gave you to me. I will make a record of the amount, and when you need money for any purpose, for clothes or bus fare or personal supplies like toothpaste or soap, you will tell me what you need and I will give you the appropriate amount out of your own funds."

Zhongmei watched as Comrade Tsang surveyed the room, fixing a brief stare on each girl as if to imprint the rules into their heads. When Zhongmei felt Comrade Tsang's eyes reaching her, she swallowed involuntarily.

"Second," Comrade Tsang resumed, "at no time is anyone allowed to leave the school grounds without permission, except for the time between the end of class on Saturday afternoon and Sunday evening, when you are free to go. If you have family or friends in Beijing, you may stay with them Saturday night, though you must report to me where you are going, and I will give you your bus fare out of your personal funds. Except for these family visits, you must never go anyplace outside the school alone. You must always be accompanied by at least one classmate, even if it's just to go to Taoranting Park across the street.

"Third, meals are to be taken in the cafeteria and only in the cafeteria. No food can be brought into the school, ever.

"Fourth, from Monday to Saturday, school days, everybody will wake up at six in the morning and will go to bed at nine at night, when the lights will be turned out. Nobody is to leave the dormitory between the hours of bedtime and wake-up. If anybody is caught outside the dormitory at that time, even in another part of the school, that person will be expelled.

"Is that clear?" Comrade Tsang again glared at the girls, who stood in a cluster in the middle of the room.

"Good. You will be orderly and decorous at all times. There will be no loud talking or rough behavior—ever. Every girl will be neat and clean. You will make your own bed in the morning. You will shower in the evening. All shoes are to be placed under the lower bunk. All clothes are to be placed in the drawers when not being worn. There are to be no clothes, books, shoes, or school supplies left lying around. Also, there is to be no talking after lights-out. You will be sure to go to the toilet before bedtime, because nobody is allowed to go to the toilet during the night. Each of you will be provided with a chamber pot, and, in case of emergency, you will use that to relieve yourself. You will deposit the contents of the chamber pot in the toilet in the morning.

"And," Comrade Tsang continued, "you will sleep facing the wall. Nobody is allowed to sleep facing out and looking in the direction of the bunks on the other side of the room. This is to discourage talking after hours. I will conduct spot checks on this from time to time, and anybody caught facing out while lying in bed will go to my office to write a self-criticism. Is that clear?"

Six girls nodded obediently, Zhongmei among them. Tsang was the most terrifying human being she had ever encountered.

"Any questions?"

Nobody dared ask a question.

"In that case, it being six in the evening, you will go to dinner in the cafeteria."

Filing out of the dormitory and across the courtyard, the girls murmured about Tsang and the rules. Zhongmei found herself next to a tall, pretty girl with long braids tied up in red ribbons.

"Hi," the girl said. "I think we're allowed to talk to each other now."

"As long as we do it quietly and with no rough behavior," Zhongmei said.

The girl smiled. "My name is Xiaolan," she said. She pronounced it *she-ow-lan*.

"Zhongmei," said Zhongmei.

"I saw you in the dormitory," Xiaolan said. "You're in the bunk opposite mine, but I guess we shouldn't be looking at each other after we go to bed."

"Or we'll have to write a self-criticism," said Zhongmei.

"But what if somebody just turns over while they're sleeping?"

"Better not do that," said Zhongmei. "You heard the rules."

"Yes, Old Maid Tsang is pretty tough," Xiaolan said.

"Old Maid Tsang?"

"Didn't you know? She's almost forty and never been married, so the students call her Old Maid Tsang."

"That's not very nice," Zhongmei said, but she couldn't stop herself from smiling. Old Maid Tsang seemed appropriate enough.

That night after going to bed, Zhongmei lay in the regulation position, facing a window next to her bunk. She was too excited to sleep and so probably were most of the other girls. They all must have heard the click as the door of the dormitory opened, and, like Zhongmei, they must all have frozen in their beds as they followed the sound of somebody's footsteps walking the length of the room and then back, until, once again, there was the sound of the door opening and closing and the

131

footsteps disappearing down the corridor outside. It had been Old Maid Tsang making her first inspection, no doubt.

Feeling that the coast was clear, Zhongmei, still wide awake, slowly turned her head to look into the room, knowing that she was already breaking the rules. The light from a streetlamp outside that filtered through the dormitory window cast the bunks across from her in an eerie pale glow. It seemed to her, though she couldn't be sure, that Xiaolan had also turned her head and was looking in her direction. Zhongmei wiggled her fingers and in the semi-darkness she saw that Xiaolan wiggled her fingers in response.

Then one of the girls started laughing softly to herself. The other girls started to laugh also, until the whole room was filled with a kind of stifled hilarity, each girl sure that to be caught laughing would mean immediate expulsion from the school and yet unable to stop. Zhongmei, choking back her giggles, turned her head back toward the wall and tried to think of something sad, like how much she missed her family, but the more she tried not to laugh, the more she laughed, until her stomach and sides ached and she thought she would die from a lack of air. Old Maid Tsang, she said to herself over and over until, finally, after a good long while, the choked-back giggles died down, and the six girls in dorm room number one went to sleep, all of them facing a wall.

13

"Six Years to Go!"

The morning bell came, as promised, at exactly six o'clock. Zhongmei climbed down from her upper bunk and dressed in a pair of cotton pants and knit pullover that each girl had been given the day before. She splashed water on her face in the bathroom, which was at the end of the corridor outside, made her bed, folded her pajamas, and put them in her drawer. Little Zhou, the girl who had helped her get settled the day before, appeared at the dormitory doorway carrying a box full of what looked like clear-colored plastic sheets. "These are your *jian fei ku,*" Zhou said—weight-loss clothes. "Find a size that fits you and put it on over your regular sweats," she said, "and then go downstairs to the outside courtyard for morning exercise." Zhongmei grabbed a set of the strange plastic clothes and pulled it on. It fit tightly at the neck, the wrists, and the ankles and made a funny crinkly sound as she ran down the stairs with the other girls, joining the six girls from dorm room number two, and running into the first-year boys, who were

133

bounding out of the first-floor corridors in identical plastic suits.

"Form a line," an instructor told the assembly in the courtyard. It was a clear, bright day, already warm. Zhongmei heard the steady sound of bicycle bells and the intermittent roaring of buses outside the gate. All the students of the school seemed to be there, from the youngest, like Zhongmei, to teenagers, and the courtyard was full. "Hold the hand of the person in front and the person in back, go out the gate and across the street to Taoranting Park," he called. Zhongmei looked for Xiaolan and grabbed her hand and the hand of another girl, and went across the street to the park entrance. The instructor led them across an esplanade on one side of the park to a lake. It was a beautiful sight, the lake sparkling in the early-morning light, willows and chestnut trees lining its distant shores. A narrow paved roadway went around the lake under the canopy of trees. On the left, an arched bridge soared over a narrow inlet.

"Everybody is now going to run once around the lake, and that's what you'll do every morning," the instructor said. "But running for dancers is not the same as running for other people. We run like this," he said, and he demonstrated a kind of leaping, prancing motion. "Go as high with each step as you go far," he said, jumping off his left foot, extending his right leg, and coming down on his right foot in a sort of jeté. "We don't so much run around the lake as we leap around it, like antelopes, or kangaroos, or, if you prefer, frogs. So now, go!"

Zhongmei began bounding down the path as instructed.

At first it was fun to leap high, her pigtails flying and brushing the low-hanging willow branches. Even the crinkling sound of her plastic suit seemed sort of funny. But by the time she'd reached what she estimated to be the halfway point around the lake, she had realized why the plastic was called a weight-loss suit. She was sweating profusely underneath it, and before long her heavy cotton pants and jersey were soaked through. The morning was still cool, but she was broiling, running out of breath, and wondering if she was going to make the whole distance, which was longer than it had first looked. I'm skinny as it is, she thought. Why do I have to wear a weight-loss suit?

After another couple hundred yards, some of the first-year students had stopped and were leaning against trees, red-faced, panting, and holding their sides. Zhongmei kept going, lumbering over the arched bridge, gasping for breath now, the pain in her side almost unbearable. It felt as if her insides were about to erupt. Her thighs burned. When she got back to the park entrance, her legs were so tired, she wished somebody would carry her back across the street.

"Now," the instructor called out, "to the courtyard for calisthenics."

"Calisthenics?" Zhongmei moaned to herself. "I'm going to die."

But she did the calisthenics too, grimacing through the pain, her body heating up still further inside her suit, the sweat pouring down her face, stinging her eyes, making her hands slippery. Jumping jacks were first, done to an accompaniment of military-sounding music that blared over an outdoor

loudspeaker, then deep knee bends, stretching movements forward, to the sides, and back, followed by sit-ups and push-ups
on the none-too-spotless courtyard ground. Zhongmei groaned,
though not more loudly than many of those around her. She
was straining so hard it was almost funny. When she'd done
fifty push-ups, at least half of which were weak upper-body
thrusts, not real push-ups, she breathed a sigh of relief, only to
find out that she wasn't finished yet.

"Leg kicks," the instructor said. "There are three kinds, so
watch carefully. First, forward kicks, like this," and he kicked
his foot up in front of his face to a level well above his head.
"Side kicks are second," and the instructor kicked first his right
leg up and to the side, then the same with the left. "Third is the
circle kick," and he kicked up and forward with his right leg,
describing a clockwise arc whose high point was about a foot
above his head. As his foot passed the middle point of its upper arc, he reached up his hand so that foot and hand slapped
loudly together. This was followed by a counterclockwise motion with the left leg and another slap of foot and hand. "With
each kick you advance a little bit, so that you kick your way
from one end of the courtyard to the other.

"Do it!" he shouted, and then led the way, once across the
courtyard with forward kicks, then back with more forward
kicks, and then two more round trips, one for side kicks and
another for circle kicks. This was no longer funny. Zhongmei
gulped air, but no matter how much she gulped, she couldn't
seem to get enough. Her sides were howling in protest. She
could feel the blood throbbing in her temples. Her heart was
racing so fast she feared it would leap out of her chest. By the

end, her kicks, which had started nicely at head level, were barely above her waist and utterly out of reach of the hand upraised to meet her foot, but, thankfully, everybody else seemed to be in about the same condition.

The exercise over (until the next day! Zhongmei reminded herself), Little Zhou led the first-year girls up the stairs to the dormitory, where they were mercifully allowed to get out of their weight-loss suits and change into dance clothing, baggy blue shorts and light blue tops.

Zhongmei listened to the commentary around her. "I can't move," one girl said. "I feel like I was left out in the rain for a month, I'm so soaked," another one said. "My feet are killing me," a third girl said. Zhongmei remembered the woman who told her during the auditions that the Dance Academy would be the hardest thing she ever did, and only now did she understand what she meant. "Only six years to go!" yelled a girl, and all of the first-year students collapsed in a combination of exhaustion and laughter.

"Breakfast first, then ballet class," Little Zhou announced, and the girls went in a bunch down the stairs and across the courtyard to the cafeteria. Zhongmei poured a glass of cool water down her throat and then devoured some *man-tou*, steamed bread dipped in tangy shrimp paste. She drank a bowl of warm soybean milk mixed with a bit of sugar. She had a second bowl and another *man-tou*. And at precisely eight o'clock, still swallowing her breakfast, she followed Little Zhou back across the courtyard to the classroom building and up a flight of stairs to the second floor and studio two, for the class called fundamentals of ballet.

14

The Country Bumpkin

"*G*ood morning, girls." A woman teacher greeted them after they'd filed into the studio. "My name is Zhu Huaimin," she announced, "and this class is the single most important dance class you will ever take at this school, as important as all the other classes put together, because here you will establish the foundation for everything else that you will do at this school. I will expect every one of you to follow my instructions and to work very hard, and if you do, I can guarantee you that you will be ballet dancers of international caliber, among the best in the world."

Zhongmei recognized Teacher Zhu right away. She was the thin, severe-looking woman with the plastic glasses who had sat next to Vice Director Jia on that day when Zhongmei had done her blade-of-grass improvisation, the one who had looked angry at the decision to give Zhongmei a second chance.

She sat on a wooden chair while the twelve eleven-year-old girls sat on the floor in front of her. "You will arrive promptly at eight o'clock every day, Monday to Saturday," she said. "You will be on time. Any person arriving late will not be allowed to take the class that day. Three times late without a medical excuse and you will be expelled from school. We will practice here for one hour every day, and then you will go off to your regular schoolwork and your other activities."

Teacher Zhu asked each of the girls to announce their names and where they came from, and Zhongmei noted that all of the girls came from big and famous cities like Shanghai, Hangzhou, Tianjin, Qingdao, and Beijing itself. When it came her turn, she gave her name and said she was from a state farm in Heilongjiang Province called Baoquanling. There were barely audible twitters from some of the other girls, and Zhongmei thought—but she wasn't sure—that she heard somebody whisper the Chinese words *tu bao zi*, which is the common term in Chinese for a country bumpkin, a hick, a rube, a local yokel. Zhongmei looked up at the semicircle of other girls to see who had whispered the phrase, but all she saw were portraits of goody-two-shoes innocence looking back at her. And yet, she had heard titters and whisperings. Why did they seem to think she was a little bit ridiculous?

But that wasn't the worst. The worst came with an incident so strange and unlikely that it's hard to believe it really happened, but it really did. As they introduced themselves, a couple of the girls boasted of having performed on television in their hometowns.

Now, in Chinese the expression for being on television uses the same figure of speech as English does. You go *on* television;

139

you are seen *on* television. But to Zhongmei, who had never watched television before arriving in Beijing, it seemed that the people she saw on television were *in* the television, not on it. And so, innocently, she asked the obvious question: "Why would anybody ever go on a television?"

There was a stunned silence in the studio followed by tittering, followed in turn by knowing looks exchanged among some of the other girls, though, again, when Zhongmei looked up, all she saw was a solid phalanx of goody-two-shoes expressions.

"What kind of question is that?" Teacher Zhu asked finally. "What's so strange about going on television?"

"You mean some of you do a dance on top of your televisions?" Zhongmei naïvely asked.

That comment was followed by another terrible silence in the room, a silence that seemed to emanate from the darkened countenance of Teacher Zhu.

"You have the temerity to make fun of this class?" Teacher Zhu said angrily. Zhongmei looked up at her. The lenses of her glasses reflected images of hanging fluorescent lights. "Do you think this is some kind of joke?" But it wasn't a question. It was an accusation.

Zhongmei felt heat on her neck, as if somebody had just pressed an iron there, and then, suddenly, it was as if she had passed through a current of freezing air. Her skin pricked. Her heart seemed to ice up. "No," she said meekly, understanding that she had done something wrong but not knowing what. "I wasn't—"

"Do you think the Beijing Dance Academy is a place for disrespect of your teachers?" Teacher Zhu said.

"No," Zhongmei said, confused because she had meant no disrespect. She was only asking a question.

"How dare you behave this way in my class," Teacher Zhu roared.

"But I didn't mean to . . ."

"You didn't mean to," Teacher Zhu said, mimicking Zhongmei's timid and frightened manner. "Then would you explain your comment, please."

Zhongmei hesitated, knowing that all she could do was repeat the question that had gotten her into trouble in the first place.

"I just asked why anybody would get on a television," Zhongmei said finally, having thought of no other way to reply.

"I will not have this!' Teacher Zhu roared, her face red, her mouth contorted in anger and astonishment. "You will get out and stand in the hall and you will stay there until you learn to behave!" she shouted, her voice both harsh and piercing, the reflection in her glasses lurid and terrifying.

There was no tittering now. All the girls stared at the floor, each of them glad it wasn't she who had aroused Teacher Zhu's ire, but each of them a little nervous that she might be next. Except for one girl. Zhongmei noticed Xiaolan, Little Orchid, looking at her in what seemed genuine concern, or maybe it was only that she looked sad compared to the other girls, who were making efforts to frown with disapproval.

"But," said Zhongmei, "I only wanted to know—"

"But nothing!" shrieked Teacher Zhu. "Get out!"

Zhongmei sat for a second, too stunned to obey this extraordinary and unjust command.

"I told you, out of the room," Teacher Zhu said. "What are you waiting for?"

Zhongmei pulled herself to her feet. Before she turned to the door, she glanced at Xiaolan, who mouthed the words "Don't worry" in an effort to give Zhongmei some comfort. As Zhongmei walked out of the classroom, Teacher Zhu's final words followed her like an angry dog nipping at her heels. "Stand outside in the corridor," she said, "and stay there until class is dismissed. I won't have anybody showing such disrespect."

Zhongmei went into the dark and gloomy corridor. A streaked window at the end let in some gray light. A portrait of Chairman Mao looked down at her from the wall and seemed silently to scold her. How could the bright and happy prospect she had felt only minutes before have turned into the misery of this dingy corridor? Zhongmei stared at the worn wooden floor. This was her first day of her dream of attending the Beijing Dance Academy and it had suddenly turned into a nightmare. She held back her tears even as the gray of the Beijing autumn entered into her heart.

That night, Xiaolan stood in front of Zhongmei's bunk and said, "I'm sorry Teacher Zhu was so mean to you."

"All I did was ask why that other girl went on a television," Zhongmei said. "What did I do wrong?"

Xiaolan explained the phrase *on television* and what it meant. "She thought you were mocking her," Xiaolan said, speaking of Teacher Zhu. "She should have understood that you just didn't know about television. I understood that, but she didn't."

"Now I've made her into my enemy," Zhongmei said. "Now I've made her hate me."

"It's not your fault," Xiaolan said. "Don't worry. She'll like you when she gets to know you."

Zhongmei shrugged and sat at the edge of her bed. She was glad that Xiaolan had spoken to her, but also ashamed at having been so stupid, the only girl in the class who didn't know what it meant to go on television.

"Look," Xiaolan said brightly. "I have something to show you."

She walked over to her own bunk, took a book from the small table next to it, and brought it back to Zhongmei. It had black-and-white pictures of a beautiful ballerina in a frilly white costume doing a perfect arabesque, her raised leg pointing diagonally upward, the knee slightly bent, her other foot planted on the ground in perfect pointe position. Her left arm balanced her raised leg. Her fine hand was opened as if she were striving to grasp something just out of reach. It was the most beautiful picture that Zhongmei had ever seen.

"Where did you get it?" she asked Xiaolan, forgetting Teacher Zhu and her worries for the moment.

"I got it from the library," Xiaolan said.

"The library?"

143

"Yes, right here. There's a library on the first floor. We're allowed to take books to our room."

Zhongmei held the book in her lap and scrutinized the picture. "What's her name?"

"That's Margot Fonteyn," Xiaolan said, though she pronounced it in the Chinese way so it sounded like *Ma-luo-ge Foh-en-tan*. "She was a great dancer, very famous, everybody loved her. Look, there are more." She flipped the pages and Zhongmei saw other dancers in poses of perfect loveliness. One especially caught her eye. It showed a girl of the most refined and exquisite features wearing a kind of village costume laced at the front and ending in a fringed skirt that flew wildly around her. One hand was on her hip, the other splayed outward, the fingers parted. The dancer's hair was bound in a piece of cloth and hung nonchalantly over her shoulder.

"That's Suzanne Farrell," Xiaolan said, pronouncing it *Su-sa-nah Fa-er-le*.

"She's great," Zhongmei said.

"Someday you'll be just like her," Xiaolan said.

"Oh, I don't think so. Not after today," Zhongmei said, but her heart was already beating quickly at the hope that, maybe, somehow, Xiaolan might be right.

"*You'll* be like her," Zhongmei said, "not me."

"I hope I will too," Xiaolan said, "but so will you."

"How can you know that?" Zhongmei asked, wishing that Xiaolan had a good reason. And she did.

"Because I heard about what you did at your improvisation,"

said Xiaolan, "after they let you try a second time. Everybody said you were amazing."

"Oh, I wasn't amazing," Zhongmei said, deeply flattered. "So many of the other girls were better than me."

"I can tell just looking at you," Xiaolan said with conviction. "I can see it in your eyes, and one of these days everybody will see it, even Teacher Zhu."

> Dear Da-jie,
>
> The ballet teacher doesn't like me, but I have a nice friend. Her name is Xiaolan, and she's the prettiest girl in my class. I wish you could come to Beijing to see me. I also wish we had television in Baoquanling. It would have saved me some trouble. Do you think you could come to Beijing? You could sleep at Policeman Li's house.
>
> Zhongmei

15

Banned from Ballet

The sun was already bright and streaming through the high windows of studio two the next day as Zhongmei and the other girls, having gotten through the sweaty, agonizing ordeal of the morning run and calisthenics, filed in for fundamentals of ballet. Even Chairman Mao, looking down on the scene from his honored place on the wall, seemed to be smiling.

"Good morning, good morning," Teacher Zhu said as each girl came into the room, and each girl in turn recited a respectful, "Good morning, Teacher Zhu."

"Everyone to the barre!" Teacher Zhu commanded, and the girls scurried for places along the wall. Zhongmei scurried for a place, noticing as she reached the barre that there was a piano in the studio and the same accompanist she had seen at the audition.

"That's fine," Teacher Zhu said, and she walked slowly along the line of girls, looking at each one. But when she came to Zhongmei, who was near the end of the line, she said, "You, come with me," and walked to a corner on the other side of the studio from the piano.

"You sit here," she said, and she pointed to a spot on the bare wooden floor.

Zhongmei looked at her uncertainly.

"You sit down here for now," Teacher Zhu said, and she pointed again to the floor.

Not understanding, and thinking that Teacher Zhu was going to tell all of the girls to take a place on the floor, Zhongmei settled down on the cool, hard wood. She watched as Teacher Zhu walked to the middle of the studio, faced the other girls, and said, "Everybody, listen carefully. Face the barre in *ding zi bu*"—basic position—"one foot straight, the other foot pointing at the first with the heel, like a *ding-zi*"—a nail. She walked down the row of girls, adjusting a foot position here, pushing in a bottom or lifting a chin there.

"The Beijing Dance Academy trains professional dancers, not amateurs, so the first thing you have to do is forget everything you've learned until now, because what you've learned until now was full of mistakes," Teacher Zhu said. "We stress Russian ballet here, but we add in many elements from Chinese classical dance. In my day I was the best ballerina in China. I studied in Moscow. I danced with the Bolshoi Ballet there. But when I came back to China, I blended what I learned with the best elements of our own tradition. There is a reason why I am your teacher in the fundamentals of ballet class.

"Now, face the barre and hold it lightly with both hands—

chin up, shoulders down, *pi-gu*"—behind—"in, not sticking out, but in a vertical line with the back of your feet. All the weight on your heels, which should feel like they're dug into the ground so that if you got hit by a car and your legs are sliced in half, your heels would still be planted there like fence posts."

Again, while Zhongmei watched from her spot on the floor, Teacher Zhu surveyed the line of girls. "OK, not great, but not disastrously bad either." She nodded at the accompanist, who began to play. "Everyone plié," she said, speaking over the music, "like this." She demonstrated a perfect half plié, and then watched as eleven of the twelve girls followed suit. "Back straight, *pi-gu* straight down, not pushed back—that's very important if you want to look like dancers rather than clowns." She curtsied, straightened, and then bent her knees, holding her back straight in the classic position.

"That's it. Curtsy, on pointe, demi-plié, and, again, on pointe. *Bu tsuo*," Teacher Zhu said—not bad.

Zhongmei looked on in amazement. Was she to sit there while all the other girls were given the ballet class? Was her punishment for her gaffe of the previous day continuing? She sat and waited, hoping that Teacher Zhu would still summon her to the barre maybe for the second half of the class. This must be some mistake, Zhongmei said to herself. She can't want me just to sit here.

The class proceeded. Teacher Zhu went over the eight directions of the body, the five positions of the feet. The girls now alternated between demi-pliés and full pliés; they practiced what American ballet girls learn as battements tendus, because in the United States we use the French terms for the various ballet steps and movements, though in China these terms have been translated into Chinese. While the other girls did their first arabesques and jetés, Zhongmei sat on the floor in a corner of the room, listening to the music and watching in mystified sadness, the tears welling up in her eyes.

"It's like somebody is taking your foot and throwing it," Teacher Zhu said, "and the rest of your body follows. But here is the difference between Russian ballet and our ballet, because we have altered Russian ballet, made it our own. In Russian ballet, the body is straight, but in China, the body is gracefully curved." Teacher Zhu demonstrated this with the step known in the West as the fouetté en tournant, where the dancer makes a full turn on her heel, snapping her head forward so that it stays facing front. "In Russia, Europe, and America," Teacher Zhu said, "the dancer turns clockwise. In China, we turn the other way. We raise our left foot like this," and she held her foot to a point just above the knee and pointed it backward, "and we follow it around, not moving our heads, so that it is much more difficult to know when a full circle has been completed." She did a turn, her narrow figure arching backward, in the classical Chinese pirouette.

"But that's just a foreshadowing of what's to come, girls," Teacher Zhu said. "We won't get to that for months. It's just something to keep in mind as an objective. Right now, class is dismissed, until tomorrow."

"I'm sure she'll let you take the class tomorrow," Xiaolan said as the two girls looked at the pictures of Margot Fonteyn and Suzanne Farrell in the dormitory that night. The rest of Zhongmei's first day had, at least, been better. After the ballet class, there had been a few hours of regular schoolwork—reading, writing, and math—and then there was a class in Chinese dance, where Zhongmei was treated the same as the other girls. Gymnastics followed that, and then *wu-shu*, or martial arts, since in China several dance forms involve acrobatic fights like the ones you've probably seen in kung fu movies.

Zhongmei did fine in those classes too. But her sleep was nonetheless troubled at night as she remembered how she had been made to sit in the corner in fundamentals of ballet while the other girls went through their movements at the barre. Would she be allowed to take the class the next day? How long would this punishment last?

The next day, Teacher Zhu allowed Zhongmei to take her place at the barre, but after just a few minutes she said, "You don't look very strong today; are you feeling sick?" And though Zhongmei protested that she felt fine, Teacher Zhu insisted that she go to the nurse, and by the time she got back—the nurse having given her a clean bill of health—the class was over. As the days of September went by, Teacher Zhu would occasionally and without explanation allow Zhongmei to take the ballet class, criticizing her harshly to be sure, but she criticized, mocked, and harangued the other girls too, so Zhongmei didn't feel bad, as long as she was at the barre with everybody else. But most days, Zhongmei would line up at the barre only to see Teacher Zhu signal to her to go to the corner and sit. Teacher Zhu often sent Zhongmei to the nurse, saying that she didn't look very healthy, and the nurse always told her there was nothing wrong with her. Sometimes Teacher Zhu would tell her to step into the corridor and practice some simple movement by herself, which meant, of course, that Zhongmei couldn't see the movements that the other girls were doing. When that happened, she would ask Xiaolan or one of the other girls to show her what she had missed, and in the time between dinner and lights-out, she would try to practice those movements. At times, when class resumed the next day, Zhongmei did those very movements, prompting a surprised Teacher Zhu to exclaim, "How did you learn to do that?" But Teacher Zhu refused to accept that as proof that she was able to take the ballet class. After a few minutes, the teacher would say, "You look tired. Why don't you take a spot on the floor and just watch for a while."

Her life was divided between the agony of her exclusion from fundamentals of ballet and the pleasure she took in her other classes. To be sure, the daily routine was exhausting, but it was exhausting for everybody. The woman at the audition had warned Zhongmei that she would be so tired at bedtime that she would almost not have the energy to wash and change into her pajamas. But Zhongmei didn't complain about that, not even secretly to herself, and much of what she did every day thrilled her. She especially loved the graceful movements of traditional Chinese dance, which the girls practiced over and over again in the afternoon classes. For weeks at a time, they would spend an entire class rehearsing just one or two of the hand movements of Chinese dance, or the special way of walking, or a single signature movement of one of the characters in Chinese opera, the soldiers, the emperors and empresses, the clowns, the princesses and prime ministers, and the character known as the monkey king, whose acrobatic leaps and somersaults had thrilled Chinese audiences for centuries. Zhongmei took to all of that naturally and her teachers praised her for her hard work and talent, so that she would finish her day happily enough, until she would remember that the next day, after the sweat-inducing run around Taoranting Lake and the calisthenics and kicking exercises in the courtyard, she would again suffer ignominiously in a corner on the floor in fundamentals of ballet.

After Zhongmei had been at the Dance Academy for a few weeks, she screwed up the courage to ask Teacher Zhu why she was so rarely allowed to take the ballet class.

"Is it because of my mistake about going on television?" Zhongmei said. "I really didn't—"

"Oh, no, it's not that," Teacher Zhu interrupted, seeming suddenly almost friendly. "I'd forgotten all about that. It's because you're not ready for this class," she said. She peered down at Zhongmei for a long minute through her plastic glasses, cocked her head, and then turned to walk away.

"But I can do it as well as the others," Zhongmei protested.

Teacher Zhu turned back and glared.

"No," she said. "You can't. I can see that already. First of all, you're not strong enough. I always feel you need to see the nurse. I've had experience with you country girls before. You just don't have enough . . ." she stopped to search for a word.

"Refinement," she said at last. "You don't have refinement. You're too coarse for ballet. You can do folk dancing and minority dances and maybe even Beijing Opera dances," she said. "They're easy enough for you. But ballet? No. Ballet involves the sublime, and the sublime is out of reach for country girls."

"But I *can* do ballet," Zhongmei insisted. "I did ballet in my hometown."

Teacher Zhu only laughed. "Yes," she said, "I can just imagine the ballet company in . . . what's the name of the place you come from?"

"Baoquanling," Zhongmei replied meekly.

"Yes," Teacher Zhu resumed. "I can just imagine the clumsy imitation of real ballet they must do there." She laughed some more, greatly amused at the very idea of a ballet company in Baoquanling, and then she walked briskly away.

16
Ice Sticks

School was six days a week for the girls and boys of the Beijing Dance Academy, and almost every minute was scheduled—the six o'clock wake-up, the run in Taoranting Park, the calisthenics in the courtyard—about seventy girls from all six of the school's grade levels on one side, an equal number of boys on the other. The boys, whose dormitory was on the first floor, did a few activities together with the girls, including the run around the lake in the morning and all the academic classes. They took their meals in the same cafeteria at the same time, but they tended to eat at separate tables. All the dance classes were separate also. During off hours, the boys tended to spend time with other boys, and the girls with girls.

After breakfast came both the dance and regular academic classes, with a break in the middle for lunch and a nap. Dinner was from five-thirty to six-thirty, and then came what a lot of the students thought was the hardest part of an already hard day. For two hours, they exercised, stretched, and practiced. The girls spent almost an hour on leg exercises alone. They would kick a leg straight up in front of them, catch hold of it with their hands at the highest point of its arc, pull it to their forehead, and hold it there until the pain was unbearable. Then they would do the same exercise to the side, pulling their legs up by the calves, holding them to the sides of their head so that their toes would tangle with their hair. And finally they would throw their legs back, pull them to the backs of their heads, and hold them for as long as they could bear it. After that, they lay on their stomachs and simultaneously raised their chests and their legs off the floor and then down again—fifty times. They lay on their backs with their legs ramrod straight, kicked them upward together while jackknifing forward from the waist so they could slap their feet with their hands—one hundred times every night.

Almost no activity was unconnected to dance. The girls rarely walked up the stairs in the dormitory or classroom building in the ordinary way, alternating feet. They hopped up stairs on one foot and then the next time on the other foot, so as to strengthen the muscles in their legs. Stretching was perpetual. The girls ate their meals standing, one leg on the ground, the other stretched across the table in front of them. They bent over the stretched-out leg and between bites they touched foreheads to their toes. In their academic classes—Chinese, calligraphy, and math—they sat at desks like any other middle school students. But when they did homework, they would stretch like they did at meals, legs thrust across a table, heads hovering over their books. This regimen caused a lot of pain. Muscles ached with fatigue.

When it came time to go to sleep, the girls were so tired

that they protested having to shower and change into their pajamas. They just wanted to flop down and sleep, sleep, sleep, and they had no energy left for clandestine giggling. Obediently they faced the wall. Sometimes Zhongmei would awaken. Once or twice in those first few months she heard the door open and somebody come into the room. The first time, she very quietly turned her head just enough to see Comrade Tsang walking between the rows of bunks, peering at each sleeping girl, making sure she was in the regulation position. One night not long after that, she was awakened by a scuffling sound, and she saw Comrade Tsang leading two of the girls out of the dormitory. In the morning, she found out that Comrade Tsang had caught them whispering to each other after lights-out, and she made them go to her office right away to write self-criticisms.

But nobody complained. Everybody understood that this was the price that had to be paid to go to the Beijing Dance Academy. Whenever she got discouraged or felt she couldn't go on, Zhongmei remembered the warning she had gotten during the auditions that this would be the hardest thing she would ever do. She had said then that she was ready for it, and that was that. She was.

Only on Saturday afternoons and Sundays did they get a little break, but only a little one. Once a month or so, Policeman Li came to pick Zhongmei up on his motorcycle and whisked her off to his house for a home-cooked meal and a sleepover. These were the times when Zhongmei could relax a little and forget her troubles. The truth is Policeman Li and Da-ma did their best to spoil her. Da-ma cooked dumplings, which Zhongmei loved. She refused to allow Zhongmei to help, or even to clean up. "You need to take it easy," she'd say.

In the evening, sometimes they would go to the movies, Policeman Li, Da-ma, Zhongmei, and occasionally Li Guang. But one evening Policeman Li and Da-ma told Zhongmei they had something special for her, and they wanted it to be a surprise. They took a bus to Wang Fu Jing, Beijing's main shopping street, where the big Number One Department Store was. But they didn't go there. They walked to a darkened part of the street to a small theater, and Zhongmei saw a sign advertising an opera called *The Zhao Family Orphan*. She settled back to watch. A man with a long black beard and a fantastic red costume appeared on the stage to a crescendo of wooden clappers and cymbals. Two officials, Zhao and Tu, are enemies of each other, and they vie for the emperor's favor, each giving him advice that is the opposite of the other's. Zhongmei and every other member of the audience can tell from the way the two men speak and the advice they give that Zhao is the good official while Tu is a conniving and mendacious flatterer. But the emperor is too vain to realize this. Not knowing which man to heed, he says he has been given the gift of a dog with extraordinary powers. It is able to distinguish good men from bad. The emperor has the dog (played by an actor in a fantastic dog costume) brought to his chambers. In a scene full of intricately choreographed movements, he allows the animal to inspect the two officials. The dog bites Zhao, and Tu, seemingly shocked, calls him a traitor and urges the emperor to have him and his entire clan of three hundred people—his wife, his children, and all of his relatives—executed.

Zhongmei gasped with horror at seeing this terrible injustice done before her very eyes. She hoped for it to be rectified, and as the opera unfolds, it is. It turns out that one of the emperor's own daughters, and therefore a princess, is married to a member of the Zhao family, so naturally she is spared the fate of the rest of the Zhao clan. The princess is pregnant. Learning this, the evil Tu plots to have the infant killed as soon as it is born. He orders one of his henchmen to do the deed, but faced with the task of murdering a baby, the henchman falters, and the child is spirited out of the palace and hidden. The years pass, and eventually the child, the Zhao family orphan (who is also the grandson of the emperor), learns what has happened, and, in a scene full of thrilling martial arts and acrobatics, of brilliantly costumed soldiers, slashing swords, thrusting spears, and deafening music, he exacts revenge on the evil Tu and his guards.

Zhongmei was enthralled. She had studied some of the movements of Beijing Opera in her class on classical Chinese dance, but she had never seen an actual opera before, and she loved everything about it, the stunning costumes, the masks, the leaps and flying somersaults, the martial arts, the clever dialogue, the tender love scenes, the many different voices, and the music, made by cymbals and gongs, flutes, mandolins, zithers, wooden clappers, *er-hus*, and other stringed instruments. Every once in a while a member of the audience, unable to contain his excitement at some especially well-executed aria or gesture, would shout out a throaty *hao!*—good—and Zhongmei found that especially thrilling. And she was mesmerized by the story of this particular opera itself, the injustice that was done, the bad judgment of the emperor, and the very long time it took for vengeance to be exacted. This was an opera, and her life was real, but wasn't she too the victim of an injustice, and didn't she too deserve revenge? Would it come? Was there a Zhao family orphan waiting for her someplace in her future? She couldn't imagine that there was, and yet the opera gave her hope that in the end justice does win out.

That night, as usual, Zhongmei was told to share a bed with Da-ma, while Policeman Li slept on the living room couch, and, as usual, Zhongmei protested.

"It's not fair," she said. "I can sleep on the couch."

"Oh, let us spoil you a little," Da-ma said. "You have a hard enough time at that Dance Academy as it is."

"I slept on the hard, cold ground when I was in the army," Policeman Li would always say. "I'm very comfortable on the couch."

"We want you to feel like this is your home in Beijing," Da-ma said. "Come anytime you want. You don't have to let us know beforehand. Just show up. We love you."

Zhongmei, fighting back tears, realized that this was the first time in her eleven years of life that anybody had ever said that to her. It wasn't that her parents didn't love her. She knew they did. It was just that with five children and such long hours of work, they never really thought to say it.

After a few weeks, Zhongmei learned how to take the bus

to the Lis' home so that Policeman Li didn't have to come to pick her up, though he always brought her back on his motorcycle on Sunday. In the first couple of months, when Zhongmei went to Comrade Tsang to ask for the bus fare, she would tell her she needed it to go to the Li family residence in the Ximen District. After a while, when she decided to spend the night with the Lis, she would simply tell Comrade Tsang, "I'm going home."

> Dear Zhongmei,
>
> I miss you too, and I wish I could go to Beijing to see you. But I think you know why I can't. Er-jie, Da-ge, and Xiao-di all send their regards. We're all fine, except that Lao Lao fell and hurt herself. It's not too serious, but her bone is broken and she has to spend a few days at the hospital. Please write her a letter. It will cheer her up.
>
> > Da-jie
>
> P.S. I've been wondering what trouble you got into there because we don't have television in Baoquanling. Whatever it was, you'll be surprised to learn that since you've been gone, we have gotten television here. It started just a few weeks ago. Of course we don't have a set, but one of the families in our lane does, so they have lots of visitors these days! There's also one at the noodle

shop in the center of town, and business there is booming!

Zhongmei didn't go "home" every weekend. The girls were expected to stay at school some Sundays in order to take part in the weekly cleanups, though they were allowed to sleep until eight o'clock, two hours later than usual. Once they were up and had breakfast, they were given assignments. Some swept the dormitory. Others dusted the furniture. Still others took the bedsheets off the beds and brought them to a laundry room for washing. The bedsheets came in pairs and were sewn onto each other, one on top and the other on the bottom of a feather comforter, so first the thread that held them together had to be removed before the girls could put the sheets into basins filled with soap and water and walk on them with bare feet to get them clean. When they were dry, they had to be sewn back onto the comforters.

That first Sunday, two of the girls accidentally sewed their own loose trousers onto the sheets, and when they got up to put the comforters back on the beds, they found they were attached to them! There were howls of dismay from the two and shrieks of laughter from the others. Then some of the others threw the sheets over the girls who had accidentally sewed themselves to them, and everybody ended up in a tangled, giggling heap on the floor.

"What is going on here!" The voice, commanding and angry, could only be that of one person. Comrade Tsang stood in the doorway of the laundry room glowering.

"Everybody, up!" she commanded.

All the girls stood at attention, Zhongmei included, but the two unfortunates who were sewed to their sheets were still tangled together on the floor.

"You two," Comrade Tsang said. "You are vandalizing state property. This is a serious offense."

"But," one of the girls began, finally managing to extricate herself from the other and to stand straight, though still attached to her sheet, which draped around her waist, "it was an accident. We sewed—"

"Be quiet!" Comrade Tsang bellowed. "I see what you've done. It was careless and stupid and it has damaged state property. You will both reimburse the school for the damage you've done."

Zhongmei swallowed hard. Reimburse the school? If she had been one of the girls who had sewed the sheets onto herself by mistake, she wouldn't have had the money for that.

Slowly, solemnly, nervously, their fingers trembling, the two girls pulled at the stitches and freed themselves from the sheets. The other girls helped. It took a long time.

"Come with me," Comrade Tsang said when the job was finished. "The rest of you, finish cleaning up at once. You saw these two girls damaging state property and all of you thought it was funny. You should be ashamed, all of you. Each and every one of you will write a self-criticism and hand it in to me before lights-out tonight."

With that, Comrade Tsang led the two more guilty girls out of the laundry room. When they returned later that afternoon, they told the others that they had had to write self-criticisms, and to turn over one yuan each for damage to the sheets.

"One yuan!" Zhongmei had exclaimed, thinking about her parents, who together made only about thirty yuan a month.

Zhongmei turned and sat at the little desk that was reserved for her schoolwork and wrote her self-criticism:

> I apologize to the Beijing Dance Academy and
> the people of China for my selfish attitude in the
> matter of sheets belonging to the school. I vow
> always to take good care of state property, which
> has been produced by the laboring masses of
> China. I promise to reform my thinking, which
> was polluted by my selfishness and my bad habit
> of thinking only about my own pleasure. I ask the
> school, the Communist Party, and the people of
> China to forgive me.

On most afternoons, those that involved no interference from Comrade Tsang, the girls who had spent the weekend at school took the bus to Tiananmen Square, and on one early Sunday, Zhongmei went along with the others. It was exciting to go there, and Zhongmei's troubled heart swelled with pride in her country when she did. She gazed anew at the magnificence of the Forbidden City, the arched marble bridges leading up to the outer gate, the immensity of the rust-red wall that extended along the whole edge of the square, the astonishing beauty and height of the curved roofs soaring above the portrait of Chairman Mao. Huge letters reading LONG LIVE THE PEOPLE'S REPUBLIC OF CHINA and LONG LIVE THE UNITY OF THE PEOPLES OF THE WORLD extended outward on either side of the gate.

This was the magnificent palace where, before modern times, only the emperor, his high officials, his wives and other family members, and their servants were allowed to set foot. Ordinary people were banned—for example, farmers' daughters from Heilongjiang—which is why it was called the Forbidden City. Now it was a museum that thousands of people visited every day. A kind of grandstand extended to the left and right, above the great red wall, and that was where China's leaders stood and watched giant parades on October 1, China's National Day, and on other holidays.

On this first Sunday excursion, Zhongmei went along to the square with about half the girls from her class. Xiaolan, who was going also, had urged her to join the little expedition. The girls dutifully went to see Comrade Tsang for their bus fare and a little money for a snack, though Zhongmei only took the bus fare. They fought their way onto a crowded bus, and twenty minutes later they were strolling on the vast esplanade.

Zhongmei wore her yellow dress, the pink blouse with the embroidered ducks, and her green shoes, and she felt people turning their heads to look at her as she passed. She thought it was because she was very pretty and very elegantly dressed, and, it is true, she was very pretty and the costume did have some elegance to it. The pleated skirt was narrowly cut and fell gracefully to her knees. But people weren't only looking because Zhongmei was pretty. What caught their eyes was the color scheme, which was just a bit too much, the yellow, the pink, the green. City people recognized it as the kind of over-done color combination that somebody from the countryside might think she should wear in Beijing, when, actually, something a bit more subdued was the fashion. The other girls wore store-bought clothing, print blouses, red scarves, cotton pants, and black cloth shoes, for example.

"Oh, ice sticks!" one of the girls shouted. A man in baggy blues wheeled a metal cart into the square. She used the Chinese word *bing-gwer*, *bing* meaning "ice," *gwer* meaning "stick." "I'm buying!" the girl said.

Her name was Jinhua, and she had been one of those who snickered most obviously at Zhongmei when she had made her error about going on television.

"We'll take turns," she cried. "Every week somebody else will invite all the others. That way it will all even out."

The ice-stick man opened the lid to his cart.

"Let's see," Jinhua said. "How many of us are there? Um . . . eight!"

"Um," said Zhongmei, "don't get one for me."

"Why not?" said Jinhua. "Don't you farm girls from Bao-quanling know what an ice stick is?" She giggled and so did some of the others. Zhongmei's ears turned red. She had stretched out the words *Bao . . . Quan . . . Ling* as if the name of Zhongmei's hometown itself was something strange and un-fashionable, like a place on another planet. Jinhua was from Shanghai, China's biggest city.

"Ice sticks aren't really sticks," Jinhua said mockingly. "They're not from trees, so don't worry, you won't have to eat bark." Some of the other girls laughed at the joke.

Zhongmei looked at the ground. She was furious at Jinhua but tried to pretend that she wasn't bothered by her mockery. There were more important things. Zhongmei thought about Lao Lao and vowed to write her a letter as soon as she got back. Who cared about ice sticks? Ice sticks weren't important. Once she had gotten poor Zhongling into serious trouble with their mother because of an ice stick, and Zhongmei remembered that time now, with yet another pang of remorse.

It happened when Zhongmei was home sick, which meant that Zhongling had to stay home from school also, like she did the time she had ruined their mother's carrot bed. In the middle of the day, Zhongmei suddenly thought how nice it would be if she could eat an ice stick. In Baoquanling, there was a small stand in the center of town where ice sticks were sold—only one flavor, a sort of milky syrup—and every once in a while, the Li children were able to have one, but it was a rare treat. But now Zhongmei felt it would soothe the soreness in her throat. The cold sweetness of it would make her happy when she wasn't feeling very good.

"I'm so hot," she had complained to Zhongling. "I have a sore throat. An ice stick will be good for me."

"An ice stick!" Zhongling said. "You know Ma and Ba won't let me spend five fen on an ice stick for you."

"But I need it," Zhongmei protested. "I have a fever. I'm burning up."

"I can't leave you alone to go get one," Zhongling said.

"Take me with you!" Zhongmei shouted. "I really want an ice stick. Please." With every second Zhongmei's craving increased until she felt she would die unless she could experience that icy sweetness, the wondrous texture of coldness melting in her mouth. She was bored at home anyway. There was nothing to do but read the book of stories she had from school, and she'd done that several times already. Needless to say, there were no toys in the Li household, no dolls or stuffed animals, no board games or trading cards or video games of the sort that Chinese kids play with today.

"Please," Zhongmei said again, as plaintively as she could.

"No!" Zhongling said.

"Yes!" Zhongmei shouted back.

"You're a greedy little girl," Zhongling said. "Anyway, I don't have five fen."

"Liar!" Zhongmei shouted. "You have money in the yogurt jar you keep in your drawer."

"Are you a spy? Keep your snotty little nose out of my things, you brat."

"I'm hot, and an ice stick will cool me down," Zhongmei replied. "Besides, it's my birthday."

"It's your birthday? Are you sure?"

Baoquanling wasn't the sort of place where a fuss was made over children's birthdays, especially in a family with five children. There was that single hard-boiled egg, and Zhongmei was expecting to get that when her mother got home that night. But there were no parties, no presents wrapped in shiny paper with smiley faces on it, no cakes, no candles, no singing

167

of "Happy Birthday," no grandparents calling from across the country. One egg—that was it, and there were years when Zhongmei's busy, harried mother forgot even that.

"What day is it today?" Zhongling asked.

"It's June twenty-seventh, my birthday," Zhongmei said.

"But you're sick," Zhongling said. "You can't walk all the way to the ice-stick stand. It's too far."

"You can take me piggyback," Zhongmei said. "Please."

"I can't carry you all the way to the town center," Zhongling pleaded. But she knew already that she had lost this battle. Zhongling loved to make other people happy. If it had been Zhongqin who was home that day, there would have been no ice stick for Zhongmei, but Zhongling didn't have the heart to disappoint her sick little sister, especially not on her birthday.

"Please," Zhongmei said yet again.

"Oh, all right."

As Zhongling carried Zhongmei all the way from their lane to the ice-stick stand in the center of town, it started to rain, and the girls had no umbrella.

"We have to go back," Zhongling said.

"After we get my ice stick," Zhongmei said firmly, tightening her grip around Zhongling's neck.

"Be reasonable," Zhongling pleaded. "We're going to get soaked."

They were already getting soaked. The rain was coming down in slanting sheets, blown by a cold wind.

"Who cares!" Zhongmei shouted. "It's fun to get wet!"

"Oh, all right," muttered Zhongling, and she trudged on.

It rained even harder on the way back, Zhongmei clinging

to her sister with one hand, holding the treasured ice stick with the other, trying to lick it fast before it got washed away. There was no shelter. It was a long walk. The rain pelted Zhongmei's hair and cheeks; it stung her eyes. Zhongling splashed through muddy puddles that formed on the earthen lane that ran to their house. By the time they got home, both girls were not only drenched, their hair matted, their shoes soaked, but Zhongmei was shivering with cold, though she kept eating her ice stick through blue lips and chattering teeth, or at least as much of it as she'd been able to save from the rain.

Zhongling helped her sister into dry clothes. She put her on the *kang* and covered her with padded blankets, muttering, "Stupid" to herself.

"Who's stupid?" Zhongmei asked weakly.

"We're both stupid," Zhongling said. "You're stupid for making such a big deal out of an ice stick and I'm stupider for taking you out of the house on a day like today. Now you're really going to be sick."

And sure enough, when the girls' parents got home, Zhongmei had such a high fever they decided to take her to the town's medical clinic, where a doctor was on duty. Zhongmei's father took her there on a bicycle cart, Zhongmei bouncing uncomfortably on the cart's bed while her mother sat alongside her, keeping her from falling off. At least it had stopped raining.

When Zhongmei was settled onto a bed in the hospital, her mother discovered that she was still holding the telltale sliver of wood left over from the ice stick she'd forced Zhongling to get for her clutched to her chest.

"Where did this come from?" her mother asked.

Zhongmei just shrugged and closed her eyes, pretending to sleep. Of all the Li children, Zhongling was the one most often in trouble with their parents, and their mother wasn't averse to administering a good spanking from time to time. Zhongmei wanted to save Zhongling from punishment. As it turned out, Zhongling didn't get spanked, but only because her mother stayed up all night with Zhongmei in the hospital mopping her brow, trying to get her fever to go down. But when Zhongmei got home from the hospital a couple of days later, she apologized to her older sister, admitted that she had been selfish, and promised never to do anything like that again.

"Have one," Xiaolan urged her now in Tiananmen. She spoke in a whisper. She thought that maybe the girl who didn't know what it means to go on television didn't know what an ice stick was. "They're really good," she assured her.

"I know they're good," Zhongmei said, whispering back, "but I don't have any money." Zhongmei's parents had given her the few yuan, Chinese dollars, left over from the purchase of the train ticket, and it had to last all year. She could use it for essential things, like toothpaste and toilet paper, which the students had to provide for themselves at the Beijing Dance Academy, and that was all. There was no fund for frivolous things like ice sticks.

"Jinhua is paying for all of us," Xiaolan whispered.

"I mean, I won't have any money to pay when my turn comes up," Zhongmei whispered back.

"Oh," murmured Xiaolan. "Well, that's all right. When it's your turn, I'll pay for you."

"I couldn't let you do that," Zhongmei replied.

"They're only five fen," Jinhua said mockingly. She had overheard. Five fen was even less than a single American penny. Zhongmei could have bought ice sticks for her entire class of boys and girls for about twenty cents, but for the family that could only eat an egg once a year, twenty cents wasn't a small amount. "Five," said Jinhua, and she spread the fingers of her right hand.

"You mean you're so poor in Bao . . . quan . . . ling . . . that you can't buy ice sticks?" said Jinhua incredulously.

"They have them once a year," another girl said.

"During the winter," said another. "In the summer they don't have ice up there."

"They have them for New Year's," a third girl put in.

"Thanks anyway," said Zhongmei. "I really don't want one."

"The farm girl is too poor to buy ice sticks!" Jinhua jeered, and the other girls, except for Xiaolan, laughed.

Zhongmei said to herself there and then that she would never again accompany her classmates on a Sunday excursion to Tiananmen, and she never did.

> Dear Lao Lao,
>
> I'm really sorry about your accident. I hope you're not suffering too much. I'm sure you'll get better quickly. You have to, because I miss you. I'm fine. The Beijing Dance Academy is

a wonderful place. I'm learning a lot, and I'm happy. I miss you very much. Please light some incense for me. Get better soon.

Zhongmei

Dear Da-jie,

   Ni hao ma—How are you? I don't feel good. My ballet teacher doesn't even let me take her class. I have to sit on the floor the whole time. She says I'm a *tu bao zi* and can't do ballet. A lot of the girls are mean. But I have one friend, Xiaolan. She always helps get lunch or dinner when I have to use that time in the studio. She always tells me that I look good. I miss you very much. Please tell Ma and Ba that everything is OK. I wrote to Lao Lao.

Zhongmei

17

Slap, Slap, Slap

The days got shorter and colder as fall tumbled toward winter. After a couple of weeks, a letter from Zhongqin arrived for Zhongmei. She tore it open and read.

> Dear Little Sister,
>   Everybody here is sad and angry to hear about the mean teacher. But we're not like her. We all believe in you—everybody in Baoquanling, the people who know you best, and of course your family. And we know that there's no fault in you. You are beautiful and graceful. And one of these days soon you will prove to everybody that you can be a star. So don't let that one person and a few silly girls discourage you. Practice as much as you can and you will do great things.
>
>   Zhongqin

The letter cheered Zhongmei up, but it also made her long for her family and her home. She dreamed of the brick house where she lived, simple and narrow but filled with the mischievous clamor of her sisters and brothers and with the smells of the soups and dishes Da-jie cooked in their little kitchen. Zhongmei used to help with the fire, which had to be lit under the stove. She would get it going with twigs, toss in a brick made out of coal, and then watch, her face enveloped in the heat, as it began to glow. The big wok would be placed on the stove, and before long it would be steaming with something fragrant. It was all so different from the fluorescent-lit cafeteria where she ate at school.

She remembered that at this time of year she would wake to a thick frost covering the wheat fields and glittering in the morning sun. She missed the *kang* that she slept on along with her brothers and sisters. At home, even when it was bitterly cold outside, the fire under the *kang* made the whole house warm and toasty, until the fire went out and everybody would wake up, covered in their heavy quilts, with the tea left over from the night before frozen in its porcelain cups. Her dormitory room in Beijing was always cold, despite the clanking, water-stained radiator under the window that was supposed to heat it.

Zhongmei missed so many things. She missed singing in front of the microphone at noon. She missed the low-slung cinder-block schoolhouse where she had learned to read and write and where no teacher bore even the slightest resemblance to the hateful Teacher Zhu, where everybody was kind and generous and full of compliments. In Baoquanling, everybody knew her and everybody liked her, and that's what she missed most of all. At night, when she thought of all those things that she missed, Zhongmei wept, muffling her tears in her pillow so that none of the other girls would hear.

One raw, wet day in the late fall, Zhongmei was not sent to her corner in fundamentals of ballet but stayed at her place at the far end of the line at the barre, happy to be included. The class began. The girls faced the barre and held it with both hands. The accompanist began tinkling out a tune on the upright piano. "As always," Teacher Zhu said, "chin up, shoulders down, *pi-gu* over your heels, stomach in, OK, and plié." Zhongmei followed directions, occasionally checking her position in the mirror on the wall opposite the barre.

"Zhongmei!" she suddenly heard Teacher Zhu calling her name. "Your *pi-gu* is sticking out so far it looks like you're looking for a place to sit down. Do you want to sit down?"

"No," Zhongmei said, not feeling too bad despite the muffled snickering of the other girls because this was the sort of ribbing that everybody got from Teacher Zhu. Teacher Zhu carried a small stick, a bit like a riding crop, that she used to slap in her open hand as she surveyed the class, so that the girls' exercises had a kind of accompaniment to them, the *slap, slap, slap* of the stick in her palm. But she also used it to slap the body parts of any dancer that were out of position, and she now employed it stingingly on Zhongmei's behind. But Zhongmei still felt happy. At least Teacher Zhu was paying attention to her, treating her the same way she treated the others.

"Well, draw it in, then, keep it over your heels, not sagging behind like a sack of rice, because if you want to sit down you can go to your spot in the corner and sit there."

The class continued, with Teacher Zhu urging the girls to keep their positions but to do it gracefully, not stiffly. Near the end of the class she went through some stretching exercises. The girls all lifted their right legs, pulled them toward their faces, and held them there, clutching the barre with their left hands.

"Up, up, up," Teacher Zhu said, and she walked down the row of girls, stinging the bottoms of their upraised feet with her stick and repeating, "Up, up, up. Get those legs higher and keep them there."

"Now," Teacher Zhu said, "left leg on pointe!" The girls lifted themselves on their left toes while their right legs remained over their heads, a maneuver that caused about half of them to let go of the raised leg, so that they had to bend over awkwardly to retrieve it.

"You girls who let go, sit down," cried Teacher Zhu. Zhongmei was among the six who were still standing. She was doing well, standing on pointe, gripping her right ankle in her right hand and pulling it straight up.

"You and you," Teacher Zhu said, tapping two of the girls on the shoulder with her stick. "You're leaning way back in order to keep your leg up. Sit down."

Four girls were left, Zhongmei among them, but the raised leg of one of them was steadily losing altitude, and Teacher Zhu told her to sit down too. Now it was Zhongmei, Jinhua, and Xiaolan, the only ones left standing. "*Bu tsuo*"—not bad—Teacher Zhu said. "Keep the leg and body straight, stay on pointe, that's it. Now, let go of the barre with your left hand."

Let go? Impossible, thought Zhongmei, but Teacher Zhu was shouting, "Let go! Let go! Let go!" as she walked along the barre ready to apply her stick to any left hand still gripping it.

Zhongmei let go. She held her position for a second and then had to grab ahold again to stop from falling, whereupon she felt the snap of Teacher Zhu's stick on her hand. She let go again, and this time, over she went right onto the floor. At first she felt humiliated, but then she saw that Jinhua and Xiaolan were on the floor too. Not a single girl had managed the whole exercise, but Zhongmei had been in the final group. She had done better than nine of the other girls and just as well as the other two. Surely Teacher Zhu would see that and allow her to take the class the next day, and the day after that.

"OK, back to the barre," Teacher Zhu said. "Final movement. Face the barre, *ding zi bu*"—basic position—"and plié." She watched as the girls followed her instructions. "Some of you are looking as stiff and awkward as elephants trying to dance," she said. "You're not holding your heads up gracefully like peacocks but stiffly like roosters crowing in the morning."

"Zhongmei!" she said suddenly.

"Yes, Teacher Zhu?"

"You're a farm girl. Make like a rooster."

"I beg your pardon?"

"What a rooster does in the morning—go ahead and do it."

Zhongmei did nothing.

"You don't know what a rooster does in the morning? You mean you're not a farm girl after all?"

"I know," said Zhongmei. It was a rare morning in Baoquanling when Zhongmei didn't hear roosters crowing at daybreak.

"Then do it," said Teacher Zhu. "How does it hold its head?"

"Like this," Zhongmei said uncertainly, and she stretched her neck and pointed her chin in the air.

"And what sound does it make?"

"Cock-a-doodle-doo," Zhongmei sang.

"You see, girls, there are some advantages to being a farm girl. Everybody look at Zhongmei. If you want to look like a rooster, you can imitate her. If you want to look like a dancer, do as I tell you."

Dear Da-jie,

I'm sorry my last letter made you feel sad. But today I'm happy. Teacher Zhu let me take her ballet class this morning, and I think I did pretty well. Only a few girls did the leg stretch without falling down, including me. Well, I did fall down, but so did everybody else, and all but two of the girls fell faster than me. I think maybe now she'll let me take the class every day.

Zhongmei

18

"You Look Like a Duck"

*B*ut it wasn't to be. "You sit on the floor and watch to-day," Teacher Zhu told Zhongmei as class began the next morning.

"Please," Zhongmei said, "I thought I'd be able to take the class today."

"I decide that," Teacher Zhu said curtly. "Sit down."

This time, instead of feeling sad and bewildered, Zhongmei felt angry. She had proved the day before that she was just as good as the others, better than most. It was time for Teacher Zhu to treat her fairly. As soon as the class was dismissed and the other girls had filed out, she caught up with Teacher Zhu at the door.

"It's not fair," she said. "I'm as good as the others, most of the others. I want to take the class every day."

"You're as good as the others?"

"I think so. Most of them anyway."

"You think rather highly of yourself, don't you?" Teacher Zhu said.

Zhongmei didn't reply. She didn't know what to say to that.

"A little bit of modesty would be very becoming," Teacher Zhu continued.

Again, Zhongmei was too dumbfounded to reply.

"I'll tell you what," Teacher Zhu said after a pause. "Let's do a little test. Think of it as an additional audition. If you pass, you can take my class every day. But if you fail, you'll let me decide when you can take the class and when you can't, and you won't bother me about this anymore. Agreed?"

Zhongmei hesitated. She knew that if she agreed, she would be falling into a trap, because Teacher Zhu would be the sole judge of this test, and, clearly, Teacher Zhu was already determined that Zhongmei would fail. But if she didn't agree, she would be admitting that she wasn't as good as the others. In any case, even if she failed, she'd just have to do what she was doing already, which was sitting in her corner.

"All right," Zhongmei said. "I'll do it."

"We have a few minutes right now," Teacher Zhu said, looking at her watch. "Go take a place at the barre."

Zhongmei took a spot.

"Listen carefully," Teacher Zhu said, standing in her usual place in the middle of studio two. "Now, *ding zi bu*, and curtsy."

Zhongmei took up first position, the nail in the ground, and curtsied in Teacher Zhu's direction.

"Not bad," Teacher Zhu said encouragingly. "Now, *er zi bu*"—second position—"and plié."

Again, Zhongmei followed instructions.

"No, no," Teacher Zhu shouted as if to a disobedient child,

curved, and lifted her leg straight in front of her and well above the level of her head, then lowered it back into fifth position. To any fair-minded person who had been watching, she would have looked like perfection itself. She was like a loose-limbed reed, her legs as supple as an antelope's, her movements as naturally graceful as a cat's. But not to Teacher Zhu.

"You look like somebody kicking a ball," she said, and she made an exaggerated motion with her leg, keeping her knee bent (when Zhongmei's had been straight) and kicking it upward, then hopping goofily backward on the other foot, her arms waving frantically to keep her balance. Zhongmei, her face glistening with tears, watched this cruel parody in silent horror.

"I didn't do anything like that," she managed finally.

"You didn't?" Teacher Zhu replied. "You think you didn't, but I was watching you, and I am not the most important ballet teacher in China for no reason!"

Zhongmei stared at the floor.

"It's no use," Teacher Zhu said. "You country girls are just not right for ballet. You just can't do it. I don't know why. Probably because you start too late. In fact, you're really not right for the Beijing Dance Academy. This isn't a place that trains pretty good dancers. This place is only for those who can be great dancers, and you're just not in that category. I don't see how you managed to get in here in the first place." Teacher Zhu seemed so upset at Zhongmei's presence at the school that she had to gasp for breath. "We were very kind to give you a second chance at the improvisation part of the audition," she said. "I was especially in favor of that. In fact, I was the one who persuaded Vice Director Jia to make an exception for you, but I can see now that I was wrong to have done that. I should have listened to him, but I was too kind. I wanted to give you a chance."

Zhongmei was dumbfounded. She remembered clearly the sour look on Teacher Zhu's face that day when Vice Director Jia told her she could try again.

"In fact, if I have anything to say about it, you won't be returning for the second year," Teacher Zhu resumed. "You'll go back to wherever it is you came from, and, believe me, my dear girl, you'll be much better off there. Much better off. Someday you'll thank me for telling you this. Oh, I know it's a little hard to hear now. Of course, you came with high hopes. I don't blame you. But I'm doing you a great kindness. I am sparing you a lifetime of futility and giving you the chance to change to something you'd be good at. Maybe you can get a part in some local song and dance troupe. Yes, you're probably good enough for that. But you'll never be good enough to dance on a national stage, and that's what we do at this school: prepare the most talented young people in China for the national stage. Someday you'll thank me for the favor I'm doing you in speaking frankly, even if I'm the only one honest enough around here to do it."

And with that, Teacher Zhu strode out the door and into the corridor, leaving Zhongmei alone in the studio to weep bitter tears. She stayed there for a little while, glad only that nobody else had been there to witness her humiliation. Or was there? Something caught Zhongmei's eye. In the narrow slit of the studio's slightly open door, she saw a single eye peering at her. The eye blinked and then quickly moved away, but Zhongmei could hear a barely muffled giggle, and she was sure she recognized the voice of her classmate Jinhua.

Zhongmei left the studio and went to the dormitory, where all the girls had to change for their sessions of regular schoolwork. She sat heavily on her bed, unlaced her pointe shoes, and threw them at the wall.

"Angry?" It was Jinhua and several of the other girls. "The farm girl is furious!" she mocked. "Let me show you all her best movement," she said to the other girls, and she kicked her leg up in a clumsy motion imitating Teacher Zhu's parody of Zhongmei in the studio. "Look what a beautiful dancer I am," Jinhua cried. She began scratching the ground like a chicken and going cock-a-doodle-doo, flapping her arms in imitation of a bird and then falling backward and sprawling on the floor, stretching her arms and legs out, howling with laughter.

Zhongmei watched, stunned. She had never hated anybody before, but now she seethed with a dark passion, wanting to destroy the cunning, sneaky little brat who was mocking her. She took a step in Jinhua's direction. Yes, she would smash the little snake into the ground under her foot. She took another step. She saw Jinhua's eyes widen. A third step. Jinhua began to back away. Zhongmei felt a firm hand on her shoulder and then an arm around her neck, warm and friendly and restraining at the same time.

"Come with me, Zhongmei," Xiaolan said. "Don't pay

attention to her. She's only doing that because she knows in her heart that you're better than she is, and she's afraid."

Xiaolan spoke softly but not so softly that the other girls couldn't hear. She put her other arm around Zhongmei and held her tight. Jinhua disappeared behind her bunk.

"Don't cry," Xiaolan whispered. "Don't let her see you cry."

"I won't," Zhongmei said.

"If you hit her, you'll surely be expelled, which is exactly what she wants," Xiaolan whispered.

"I'm OK now. Thank you, Xiaolan."

Da-jie, Zhongmei wrote.

> I've made a big decision. I know I'm going to be sent back home after this year is up. I have to accept that I'm not pretty or graceful enough for the Beijing Dance Academy. I'm the ugliest girl here. So I've decided to enjoy myself and to learn as much as possible before I go home. Some of my classmates are saying that three of us are going to be sent back, and I am one of the three for sure. But don't worry about me. I will still try my best. At least I'll be able to learn something this year and teach in my hometown, right? I'm happy that I made it this far, and I won't have come to Beijing for nothing. I am not sad anymore. I will go back and dance more as soon as I have sent this out. Don't tell Ma and Ba I'm going to be sent back.

李忠梅

19

Hungry in Harbin

*T*he fall turned into winter, and Beijing was battered by the blasts of cold air that sweep over the North China Plain every year. In the mornings, the girls' feather comforters would be covered in a fine layer of yellow dust, blown in from faraway Mongolia. The air smelled of coal burning in ten million furnaces and cooking stoves in the city. Outside, the city's sidewalks were piled high with cabbages, which people kept in great, aromatic mounds wherever they had room—in their stairwells, in kitchen sheds, along the walls that divided their homes from the street. Cabbage was the only vegetable readily available during the winter in those days in China. People pickled it with hot peppers to make a condiment called *pao tsai*. They cooked it in soup, or chopped it for dumplings, or fried it in garlic and oil, and ate it with steamed bread or rice.

Whenever the girls left the academy, even just to go to buy toothpaste at the general store down the main street across from Taoranting Park, they would see people bundled in padded cotton, waiting in long lines to get their monthly allotments of rice or, if they had small children, powdered milk. China in those days was very poor. Meat was rationed at about half a pound per person per month. Even toilet paper, which was brown and rough, was considered a luxury, and most people made do with squares of paper they cut out from the newspaper. In the early evening, as dark enveloped the city, there would be masses of people waiting curbside for a bus to take them home. And when, after what always seemed a long time, it arrived, there would be a near violent rush for the door because there was never enough space for everybody inside. Whenever she saw that, Zhongmei felt glad that she lived at the school and only took the bus when she went to spend a Saturday with Policeman Li and Da-ma, and the bus wasn't so crowded on Saturdays.

The New Year in China usually falls in late January, and when it does, the whole country closes down for a week, and so of course did the Beijing Dance Academy—a few days longer than a week in the case of the Dance Academy, to give time for out-of-town students to get home and back. It was the only time of the year, aside from a few weeks during the summer vacation, when everybody was required to go home, and, in any case, every Chinese person wants to be home for the New Year. Zhongmei packed her small suitcase and Policeman Li came to the school and took her to her Beijing home for a day of pampering by Da-ma. Then he brought her to the train station for the trip that Zhongmei dreaded, the two nights and three days on the train to Harbin, then to Jiamusi, the bus to Hegang, and another bus to her hometown, which she never wanted to leave again as long as she lived—only to have to leave again after a few days or so for the long, grueling trip back to Beijing.

As expected, the trip was awful, interminable. Because so many people were traveling for the holidays, the train stations were a pandemonium of desperate crowds of people bunching up at ticket windows, pressing together at turnstiles, scrambling to find places on trains. Zhongmei had a ticket—the Dance Academy helped with that—but to be a small girl traveling alone on China's grim and creaky transportation network was a waking nightmare. The hard-seat cars were ice cold, drafty, and crowded. The toilet was slimy and smelly. Suitcases and plastic satchels were jammed under the seats and between them, in the aisles, and on the overhead luggage racks, from which every once in a while one would get dislodged and drop down with a menacing thud. It was a miracle nobody got knocked unconscious. Zhongmei squeezed into a seat, her shoulders compressed by the two much larger people on either side of her. She managed to doze a little during the long first night as the train rumbled northward passing one brown village after another, but mostly she stayed awake, unable to sleep, yearning for the night to be over. At long last, dawn broke, and out the stained, streaked window she saw brick kilns sitting in the middle of stubbly fields, crumbling stone walls, bicycle carts, smokestacks on the horizon, and the outlines of distant hills a dark purple under the pale gray sky.

The train stopped at deserted platforms, and in the great

silence Zhongmei thought about her situation. In the last few weeks before the New Year's break, a new disappointment had been added to her life. Every morning a list went up on a bulletin board outside the cafeteria assigning the first-year girls to studios for afternoon rehearsals. These rehearsals were aimed at teaching the skills of partnering, and it was the only time in the first year when boys and girls practiced together. The students in Zhongmei's class did simple duets. The boys learned to lift and support the girls, the girls to be lifted and supported. In addition, a special group of rehearsal instructors separate from the regular faculty taught some of the basic Chinese dances, the kind that the students would perform before audiences later, and these instructors chose the students for their particular class.

On the first morning when the rehearsals were announced, Zhongmei and all the others scurried to the bulletin board to learn their assignments, but Zhongmei didn't find her name on any of the lists. This must be a mistake, she thought. She went to the school office.

"I can't find my name on the rehearsal list," she told the secretary.

"Well, none of the rehearsal teachers put it down, then," the secretary answered.

"But what about my rehearsal?" Zhongmei asked.

"You don't have rehearsal," was the response.

"What am I supposed to do during that time?"

"I don't know. Do what you want. You can watch the rehearsals through the studio door if you want."

"But why aren't I assigned to a rehearsal?" Zhongmei persisted.

"Because none of the rehearsal teachers wanted you," came the cruel response.

There was one other girl who didn't get called to rehearsals, and the rumors around the school were that she and Zhongmei were going to be sent home at the end of the year. Meanwhile, for the last few weeks before the vacation, Zhongmei and that girl, whose name was Tiehua, wandered the hallways looking in the doorways as the other first-year students rehearsed. Or they went to the dormitory and wrote letters home, like this one that Zhongmei wrote to Zhongqin:

> Dear Da-jie,
>   I'm sad today. Me and one other girl are not being chosen for rehearsal. It's because everybody knows that we're the worst ones and we're going to be sent home. But don't worry. I'm watching the others and learning what they do, so I'll be able to teach rehearsal in Baoquanling after I'm sent home.
>
>   Zhongmei

The train rumbled on for another interminable day and another night, Zhongmei feeling like a prisoner inside it. When it arrived in Harbin at dawn, Zhongmei had to wait the entire day for her connection to Jiamusi. Miserably tired already, she settled onto a bench in the waiting room. Just as she began to doze off, a uniformed attendant wearing a peaked cap and a red armband that said SECURITY on it asked to see her ticket.

"But your train doesn't leave until tonight," she told Zhongmei.

"That's right," Zhongmei said, and closed her eyes, wanting to go back to sleep.

"That's almost twelve hours from now," the security guard said.

"Yes, I have a long time to wait," Zhongmei replied.

"It's against the rules to use the waiting room for more than an hour before the departure of your train," the attendant announced coldly.

"But," Zhongmei sputtered, "where can I go?" The security guard shrugged and pointed to the station door.

Zhongmei walked the streets of Harbin, carrying her suitcase, her hands and feet growing icier by the minute, her nose so cold she feared it would freeze solid and fall off her face. People bundled in green padded overcoats with brown fur collars and hats with earflaps tied under their chins rushed by, hunched against the cold, indifferent to a small girl with a suitcase and no place to go. Buses roared and spewed plumes of black smoke into the air. Cars honked their horns to warn careless pedestrians to get out of the way. Zhongmei saw a narrow lane full of outdoor cooking stalls, steam emanating from large iron pots where noodles in soup were being prepared. She was hungry, but she had so little money she didn't dare buy a bowl for herself. Shivering, not knowing how she could last outside for the entire frigid day, she took refuge in a department store, standing among aisles of cotton padded jackets and pants.

"What are you doing here?" a tall man, evidently a salesman, asked her, not in a friendly tone.

"I'm coming from Beijing and I have to wait all day for the train to Jiamusi," Zhongmei replied.

"Where are your parents?" the man asked.

"My parents? They're in Baoquanling. They're not with me."

"Well, your parents need to take care of you," he said. "You can't just stay here all day. You have to find someplace else."

Zhongmei went back out onto the street, the cold hitting her like a wall. She wandered aimlessly into a maze of small streets of metal workshops, her feet so cold that she knew she was in danger of frostbite. How could that man in the store have been so mean to a small girl? she wondered. What harm would it have done for her to stay in the store? Her shoes were too thin, inadequate for Harbin in the middle of winter. She wiggled her toes to try to stimulate her circulation, but it was no use. Her feet were aching so much that she had tears in her eyes from the pain. Can a girl just freeze to death in the middle of a city and nobody care? she thought. She saw a group of men through a half-open doorway sitting around a table in a room with a potbellied stove. Desperate to get out of the cold but afraid to go in, she stood uncertainly on the street peering inside, until one of the men noticed her.

"You look ice cold, *xiao-mei-mei*, come on in," he said in a friendly voice. His use of the term *xiao-mei-mei*, little miss, gave Zhongmei some comfort.

The room smelled of smoke, pickled garlic, and sweat, but it was warm inside, and Zhongmei felt it was a refuge.

"What are you doing out on the streets on a day like this?" the man said. He was large and round in his blue padded suit. He had a stubble of beard and bushy eyebrows. Around the table were five or six men smoking and pouring tea out of a large red thermos into glass fruit jars with screw-on caps. Their huge green overcoats were thrown over the backs of their chairs.

Zhongmei explained that she was a student at the Beijing Dance Academy on her way home to Luobei County and had to wait all day for the train.

The Beijing Dance Academy! This impressed her new friends, and they asked her if she would do them a little dance. Zhongmei put down her suitcase. She found a little bit of space on the earthen floor in front of the stove and, warm for the first time in several hours, she performed the movements she had studied in her classes of classical Chinese dance, the hand and head movements, the princess's walk, the jerky motions of the monkey king. First-year students didn't do entire dances, but only parts of them. Sometimes whole hour-long classes would be devoted to the repetition of just a single gesture of hand or head or foot. But there in front of the coal stove on a narrow lane in Harbin, Zhongmei, humming the music, performed a whole dance, one that tells the story of a peacock transformed into a woman. When she was finished, the men applauded loudly. One of them went out and came back with a bowl of noodles in soup to give to her, and she devoured it as though she hadn't eaten in days.

The men, who were on their midmorning rest break, returned to work in the yard behind the room where she'd performed, but they told her to stay there until it was time to go to her train. What a relief! Zhongmei gratefully sat on a chair in front of the stove, listening to the metallic clang emanating from the back of the workshop, smelling the musky coal smell of the stove, feeling drowsy, warm, and safe. She knew that from then on, every time she made the long journey from Beijing to Baoquanling and back, she would go to this narrow street of metal workshops and do a little dance in exchange for a bowl of noodles in soup. She knew she would always be welcome. But that made the big question in her mind all the more vexing: Would she, after this year was over, be returning to Beijing, or would she just stay in Baoquanling, probably for life?

20
Daring to Struggle

*I*t was four o'clock in the morning. The dormitory was cold because it was too early for the radiators to provide their loud noises and paltry heat. Zhongmei was awakened by the tug of a length of string tied around her wrist. She stirred. She sat up on her upper bunk and pulled the string to let the person on the other end of it know that she was awake. Very quietly, so as not to disturb the sleep of the other girls, she climbed down and changed from her pajamas into her blue jersey and shorts, the clothes all the girls wore to ballet class. Shivering, she pulled on her cotton shoes and, oh so quietly, stole out of the room, crept down the stairs and out the door, making sure it shut soundlessly behind her. She flew like a phantom across the courtyard outside to the classroom building, the cold penetrating to her bones. She gingerly pushed open the door and felt her way up the stairs to studio two on the second floor. Once inside, she flicked a switch, turning on just one light, so it was in a semi-illuminated gloom that she stood at the barre and began to go through the movements that she had seen the other girls doing the day before in Teacher Zhu's fundamentals of ballet class.

It had been just two days since Zhongmei's return to the Dance Academy from her New Year's visit to Baoquanling, which had been eventful, discouraging, and then, in its way, inspiring. She had been welcomed like a conquering heroine. Already at the Jiamusi train station, she was surprised to find her big sister waiting on the platform along with a cameraman and a reporter for the new television station in Luobei County. The camera followed Zhongmei as she flew across the platform and threw her arms around Zhongqin. Then all four of them got on the bus, first to Hegang, then to Baoquanling, the cameraman filming along the way, the reporter asking her about the Dance Academy. Her whole family was waiting for her at the bus stop, even Ma and Ba along with her second sister and her two brothers, and quite a few other people, her dance teacher, some of her classmates from elementary school, and a few of the families that lived on the same lane as her family in Baoquanling.

Zhongmei smiled and waved as she got off the bus, realizing fully for the first time just how big a deal it had been in her hometown for a local girl to be accepted at the Beijing Dance Academy. The first thing she did that night was rush into the bedroom to see Lao Lao, who was seated in a small chair next to the kang so that Zhongmei had to kneel down to embrace her.

"I'm proud of you," Lao Lao said.

"I missed you, Lao Lao," said Zhongmei.

That night, the mayor of the town came in an official car to visit at her family's little brick house, accompanied by the television journalist who had met her in Jiamusi. Tired as she was from the trip, Zhongmei bowed as she shook the mayor's hand and thanked him for the honor of this visit to her home. She patiently answered his questions about the Dance Academy, not saying anything about her trials and tribulations there.

"We're all proud of you," the mayor told her.

"Thank you, comrade mayor," Zhongmei said. "I'll do my best to be deserving of your praise."

The next day, Zhongmei went with her parents to the Hu family, several houses down in their lane. They were among the people who had lent money for Zhongmei's train ticket to Beijing, and everybody thought Zhongmei should visit them to say thank you.

"Ai-ya!" Mrs. Hu exclaimed when she saw Zhongmei at the door. "We're just watching you on television! Come in quickly so you can see yourself."

"I should have told you," Zhongqin whispered as they went through the Hus' front courtyard, lined with roosts for chickens and ducks, just like the Lis' front courtyard. "They're the ones in our lane who have the television."

Mrs. Hu practically pushed Zhongmei into the main room of the house, where Zhongmei saw a long *kang* along one wall and, facing it on a small table, a color television, its screen glowing. As Zhongmei arrived, she heard an announcer saying, "A model performer from Baoquanling is working hard to become a star for the whole country." She watched with amazement as an image flashed on the screen showing her arrival the day before at the Jiamusi train station. She saw herself run across the platform and throw her arms around Zhongqin. She heard herself speaking into the microphone that the television journalist had held in front of her on the bus ride to Hegang. She was saying how honored she was to represent Luobei County and the Baoquanling State Farm at the Beijing Dance Academy. Next, she saw Baoquanling's mayor arrive at her house and pose for the cameraman with Zhongmei's entire smiling family.

"We're so proud of you!" a beaming Mrs. Hu cried. "You'll show them what we countryside people can do!"

That night, even though she was exhausted and craved sleep, Zhongmei lay awake for a long time on the *kang* and thought. All that attention! It was flattering, of course, a great honor. The mayor himself at their home! The cameraman and reporter at the train station. But it didn't make her happy. Quite the contrary, it increased her already heavy burden, because it brought home to her that for her to fail at the Beijing Dance Academy would be to let down the entire state farm of Baoquanling with its thousands of people excited about her being chosen. It would be an unbearable embarrassment for her family and a humiliation for her. She would never be able to show her face again. And yet, what could she do? How could she stay at the Dance Academy and succeed there if one of the most powerful dance teachers in China was against her?

She lay awake as the heat that had earlier radiated from beneath the *kang* faded and the cold from outside crept into the room. Zhongmei pulled a heavy quilt over her, but sleep just wouldn't come. She asked herself the same questions over and over: Why did Teacher Zhu hate her so much? Was it true that girls like her from the countryside just couldn't compete with the city girls? Could Teacher Zhu be right? Had she started too late and was it impossible for her to catch up? If that was true, then, plainly, she just wasn't good enough. And if it wasn't true, and Zhongmei was deeply confused on that question, what difference did it make anyway, so long as Teacher Zhu remained her enemy?

"We're all proud of you," the mayor had said, echoing Mrs. Hu and many other people. Lao Lao had said the same thing. Well, they wouldn't be so proud if she were expelled from school, would they? Zhongmei thought of a lot of things. She pictured herself sitting on the floor of the ballet studio watching the other girls in her class take the fundamentals of ballet. She remembered how she had almost been given away to neighbors when she was a baby, and now she felt that she had been given away, or at least that she was as alone in the world as she used to imagine she would feel if she had gone to live with strangers. She thought of Chinese classical dance, where her teacher always praised her. She rehearsed in her mind the movements of the peacock dance that she had done for the metalworkers in front of the stove in Harbin, and she smiled. She remembered the day she had left on the bus for Hegang on the first leg of her trip, excited and scared at the same time, the ice sticks Zhongqin had bought for her and Huping in Jiamusi, hers dripping down her fingers. She opened her eyes and looked around the room, at her family members, one after another asleep on the *kang*. The picture of Chairman

Mao that had once frightened Zhongmei surveyed the scene with those unblinking eyes.

The picture of Mao was saying something to her, something important, she felt, and she tried to grasp it, to know what it was. It was something bold, something audacious, something about turning the situation to her advantage, but what was it? Zhongmei felt the weight of the heavy quilt on her as she lay on her back and looked at Mao. Then she rolled over, closed her eyes, and, finally, fell into a deep and restful sleep.

Early every morning after that night, as the farmers of Baoquanling walked to work, they were greeted with the sight of Zhongmei jogging down the pounded earth paths between the wheat fields, except Zhongmei didn't jog exactly, she ran with the high-stepping antelope motion she used every morning as she ran around Taoranting Lake. It was icy cold in Baoquanling, and Zhongmei was bundled up in padded clothing, a green army hat with fur earflaps fastened under her chin. The air felt like powdered ice as she breathed it in great gulps, reemerging as plumes of steam. Often Zhongqin would accompany her on a bicycle, and the townspeople would see the two sisters in the middle of the flat stubbly fields silhouetted against the distant purple hills, their visible breath swirling around them.

It's a safe bet that the Baoquanling farmers who saw her running in the mornings understood that Zhongmei was in training for her regimen at the Beijing Dance Academy. What they didn't know was that she was afraid of returning in disgrace and was determined to do everything she could to avoid that fate, including this early-morning effort to stay in tip-top shape. Even the other members of the Li family were unaware of Zhongmei's secret struggle, all the members except for Zhongqin, from whom Zhongmei never kept anything.

"She wants to stop me from returning for a second year," Zhongmei said after her run was finished on her second morning back home. Zhongmei was speaking of course of Teacher Zhu. "She told me that I shouldn't have been accepted in the first place."

"I can't be sure why she's so against you, and whatever reason she has, it's a bad reason," Zhongqin said. "I hate her even though I've never met her. But I think I know the reason."

"What is it?" Zhongmei said, stopping in her tracks and looking at her older sister.

"She's from Shanghai, right?"

"I think so. A lot of the people from the Dance Academy are from Shanghai," she said.

"Well, you know, a lot of people from Shanghai look down on us people from the countryside," Zhongqin said. "They think we're all hopeless bumpkins."

Zhongmei thought of Jinhua, who was very proud of being from Shanghai, which was China's biggest and most sophisticated city.

"Also," Zhongqin continued, "people like Teacher Zhu suffered a lot during the Cultural Revolution."

Zhongmei of course had heard stories of the Cultural Revolution, which started around the time she was born, and she knew it caused a lot of suffering for a lot of people, but her family, being poor countryfolk, were pretty much unaffected by it, and she didn't understand what it could possibly have to do with Teacher Zhu's dislike of her.

"You were too young to know everything that was happening, so you don't know just how crazy things were," Zhongqin explained. "Everything was upside down. People who were rich and educated were taught by poor people with no education. If you came from a family that had, maybe, a piano or some old paintings, or if you were a university professor or maybe just a dance teacher, that meant you had to be reeducated by ordinary people, and people got reeducated by working in factories or on farms. We had professors from Harbin University right here, working in the beet fields.

"They had to work in the fields during the day and then have political education at night," Zhongqin said. "They weren't used to the hard life of the countryside. It was very difficult for them."

Zhongmei found this interesting and disturbing, but she didn't understand what it had to do with her.

"It doesn't have anything to do with you, or it shouldn't," Zhongqin said. "Anyway, that's all over now. Things have returned to normal. The professors went back to Harbin University right after the Gang of Four were arrested. But it was exactly people like Teacher Zhu whom the Red Guards attacked. If the Red Guards didn't like somebody, they could hold a big meeting, put a dunce cap on their head, accuse them of being traitors to Chairman Mao, and beat them. I don't know if that happened to Teacher Zhu, but it surely happened to lots of people she knew. And she was probably terrified."

"I see," said Zhongmei, soaking up this lesson in recent history.

"Maybe you remind Teacher Zhu of the way everything was upside down," Zhongqin continued. "She wants everything to be right side up again, and right side up means students from the best schools, students who've been on television and had ballet lessons since they were three years old, cultivated students from big cities like Shanghai, not rough country girls who don't know what 'going on television' means."

"Yes, I see," Zhongmei said. "Like that girl who talked to me on the line during the auditions once. Remember, I wrote to you about her. She told me I had no chance to get in because all the places were already taken and the audition was just a show."

"Yes, I remember when you wrote to me about her. She must have been pretty surprised when you did get in," Zhongqin said.

"I remember her name," Zhongmei said. "It was Wang Tianyuan. She said her family was very close to one of the Dance Academy teachers, and that's how she knew her name was on the list. But then she didn't get chosen."

"She didn't?" Zhongqin said. "You never told me that."

"No, her name wasn't on the list. She didn't get in. And I remember she was pretty upset about it."

"Hmmm," Zhongqin said. "I wonder."

"You wonder what?" Zhongmei asked.

"I wonder if Teacher Zhu was the teacher that girl's family knew at the Dance Academy."

"I don't know, but what if it was?"

"Well, they're both from Shanghai, right?"

"Right," Zhongmei said, still not sure where her older sister was going with this.

"Well, maybe Teacher Zhu did know this girl Tianyuan and she had promised her family that she was going to be selected, but then you got the place that was intended for her. Don't forget, in Teacher Zhu's mind, you're the clumsy bumpkin, and Tianyuan is exactly the kind of girl the Dance Academy was meant for."

Zhongmei thought about that. It was just a theory, of course, and it seemed kind of far-fetched. Could it really be that of all the thousands of girls lining up for the audition that day, she had met the very one who was favored by Teacher Zhu?

"I can't believe that could be the reason," Zhongmei said. But then she remembered the look of annoyance on Teacher Zhu's face when Vice Director Jia had given her a second chance at the audition. And she remembered word for word what Teacher Zhu had told her that humiliating day when she tricked her into doing a special audition for the ballet class, when she told her she looked like somebody trying to kick a ball. "This place is only for those who can be great dancers, and you're just not in that category," Teacher Zhu had said, and the words now reverberated in Zhongmei's ears. Then Zhongmei remembered the look on Tianyuan's face that morning when Zhongmei learned that she had been selected, and Tianyuan learned that she hadn't been. It was a look not just of hatred or of amazement, the look of somebody who's been robbed of a possession, who thinks that something that belongs to her has been taken away by somebody else.

The girls crossed a rutted path. The sky was blue, the day crystal clear. The more she thought about it, the more Zhongmei felt that Zhongqin's theory might just be right. In a way, it made her feel better, because if her sister was right, then Teacher Zhu's attitude toward her had nothing to do with what kind of a dancer she was really. It was just Teacher Zhu's preference for somebody else. But then she had a worrisome contrary thought. What if Teacher Zhu was right? What if she really wasn't in "that category," the category of the best of the best, the ones who could not just be good but were likely to be great? The thought haunted Zhongmei. But in any case it was too late. She had gotten on that bus to Hegang a half year earlier. She had started. People had lent her money to go to Beijing, and they were expecting her to prove that people like them were as good as anybody else. Whatever Teacher Zhu's reasons for picking on her, there could be no turning back now, no giving up.

"But you know," Zhongqin resumed after a pause, "you can only do your best. And if you work as hard as you can and you don't succeed, you have nothing to be ashamed of."

"But I will be ashamed," Zhongmei said. "The mayor himself came to our house to congratulate me. The picture of the whole family was in the newspaper. If I'm expelled at the end of the year and become a dance teacher in Baoquanling, I'll be known forever as the girl who didn't make good."

The two sisters were walking at the very edge of the state farm near the river that divides China from Russian Siberia, Zhongmei lifting her feet high to stretch her leg

Zhongqin wheeling her bicycle alongside her. In the distance, the sun sparkled on the Heilong River, which had iced over and was covered in a layer of ruffled, twig-strewn snow. The trestle bridge to the Soviet Union was just around the bend, though there was no traffic on it, because relations between China and the Soviet Union were very bad and the border was closed. Zhongmei stamped her foot on the hard ground.

"I tell you," she said, "I will die before that happens. I mean it. I will die."

Zhongqin knew she was telling the truth.

"But don't the other teachers like you?" she asked.

"Most of them do, yes," said Zhongmei, "especially my Chinese classical dance teacher. She's always telling me that I'm doing very well."

"And then there's Jia Zuoguang. He let you repeat your improvisation at the audition. He must like you. Surely he won't allow you to be sent packing."

"I don't know about him," Zhongmei said. "I've never even seen him since the audition. Do you think he pays attention to first-year students? Anyway, even if Teacher Zhu is my only enemy, she's very important and powerful at the school. And also, none of the rehearsal teachers want me. There are only two girls who haven't been taken for rehearsal, and I'm one of them."

Zhongmei felt tears forming in her eyes and rolling icily down her cheek.

"You just can't imagine how good the other girls are," Zhongmei said. "They're so pretty and graceful. Here in

Baoquanling, people think I'm good, but at the Beijing Dance Academy, I'm the worst."

"No, Zhongmei," Zhongqin exclaimed. "Don't let them make you think that way. Don't give up. The biggest embarrassment is to give up."

"Well, I don't want to give up, but I don't have much of a chance whether I do or not."

The truth is that it's not easy for a young girl to believe in herself with somebody like Teacher Zhu against her, telling her that her pliés made her look like a duck. Zhongmei thought of the night Xiaolan had told her that she was the best of them all, and that encouraged her, but it was hard for her to banish all self-doubt from her spirit, especially when she thought of Jinhua lying on the floor of the dormitory and laughing with derision at her. Jinhua came from Shanghai. Her father was a big official in the city government. Her mother too. She was one of the girls who had performed on television before coming to the Beijing Dance Academy. She was a haughty, nasty girl, but she was pretty and she was a good dancer. Could it be true that a girl like Jinhua belonged and Zhongmei didn't?

Reading her mind, Zhongqin said, "You told me in one of your letters that each student performs before the whole school at the end of the year. If you show everybody at the school how good you are, you couldn't be expelled, right?"

"Do well in the year-end performance? How can I do that if I can't even take the ballet class?"

"Can you take it on your own?" Zhongqin asked.

"On my own?" Zhongmei replied.

"Watch what the other girls do and practice it yourself. Go to the park on Sunday and do it there. I don't know, but don't give up. There must be a way."

"There's no way," Zhongmei said, but Zhongqin had given her an idea. A way, a possible way to avoid the worst, began to form in her mind. Show the whole school at the end of the year what she could do! Suddenly she realized what the portrait of Chairman Mao was telling her the night before. There was a phrase of his that all Chinese schoolchildren were expected to memorize: "Dare to struggle; dare to win!"

Yes! she thought. She would struggle, and maybe if she struggled hard enough, she would win. But again, how? She looked at Zhongqin, who was laboring with her bicycle over the stubbly field. Farm trucks clattered in the distance. On the horizon was the huge chimney of the power plant, a plume of black smoke soaring above it toward the clear blue sky. Baoquanling was so different from Beijing, so barren, especially at this time of year. It was so far away that Zhongmei felt it wasn't the edge of China but that it was beyond the edge, and that she and everything she knew had dropped into some abyss on the other side.

"You're right, Da-jie," Zhongmei exclaimed. "I am going to show them! I'm going to do it!"

"That's the spirit!" Zhongqin said. She walked a little further. "How?" she asked.

And Zhongmei spent the rest of the time on the way home telling her her plan.

21

A Piece of String

*B*esides Xiaolan, the other person who was friendly to Zhongmei at the school was Old Zhou, the night watchman with the wispy beard whom Zhongmei had met her very first day at the Dance Academy. Everybody called him Lao Ye, Grandpa, and everybody saw him every day as they passed through the courtyard gate on their way to the morning Taoranting jog and on their way back. After greeting students in the morning, Old Zhou would then sleep for most of the day, because his main job, keeping watch over the buildings in case of thieves or other intruders, came at night. Every couple of hours or so he would walk around the Dance Academy perimeter, between the buildings and the outer wall. At six o'clock every morning he rang the wake-up bell. Whenever he saw Zhongmei emerge into the courtyard for the early exercise, he always gave her a friendly smile.

Zhongmei thought about that smile on the terrible train ride back to Beijing, another three days and two nights of misery. She got some relief from her new friends at the metal workshop in Harbin, but on the endless trip from there to Beijing, she was so exhausted, so cramped, so desperate to lie down, that she held her nose and crawled under her hard-seat bench. There, amid the dust and grime and awful smells of the train floor with the muddy feet of the other passengers in front of her eyes, she managed a few hours of sleep. But when she woke up and crawled back out between the legs of her fellow passengers, she felt angry that she had had to do something so terrible, lying under the seat like a rat hiding on a ship. Her coat was smudged and her hair matted, and she imagined that she looked like a wreck. And there were still hours and hours to go to Beijing. With nobody to travel with her this time, Zhongmei felt her solitude painfully, and she was overjoyed when, at long last, the train arrived at the Beijing station and there was Policeman Li standing on the platform waiting for her with a big smile on his face.

Zhongmei spent one night with him and Da-ma, who took one look at Zhongmei and swept her off to the public bath down the lane so she could wash off the grunge of the trip. Zhongmei gratefully untied her pigtails and washed her hair, not once but three times, and she splashed herself with warm, sudsy water while Da-ma rubbed her down with a wet cloth. Afterward, drinking a bowl of hot soup, she felt much, much better, and yet that night, even though she lay in a clean, comfortable bed muffled in a heavy quilt, the *clackety-clack* of the train reverberated in her head and she had trouble sleeping. In the morning, knowing she had to go back to the Dance

211

Academy, she got on Policeman Li's motorcycle with a feeling of anxiety gnawing at her stomach.

When she arrived, the first thing she did, after depositing her small suitcase in her room, was to visit Old Zhou in his guardhouse.

"Lao Ye, I need your help," Zhongmei said.

"I'll do whatever I can for you, *xiao-mei-mei*," Old Zhou said.

"Can you come into the dormitory early in the morning, at four o'clock, and wake me up?"

"When? Tomorrow morning?"

"Yes, tomorrow morning and every morning after that," Zhongmei said.

"At four?" Old Zhou exclaimed. "Why on earth would you want to get up so early?" It was a reasonable question.

Zhongmei told him about her problems with Teacher Zhu.

"Oh, that one," Old Zhou said. "She's a mean one."

"I don't know why she hates me," Zhongmei said.

"Well, she's prejudiced against us ordinary people," Old Zhou said. "But what can I do to help? It would be against the rules if I came creeping into the dormitory to wake you up. If I got found out doing that, I'd be in trouble," he said.

"But I'll never tell anyone," Zhongmei pleaded. "Nobody will ever know."

"I believe you, but we'd get found out sooner or later. What if one of the other girls woke up just then and saw me shake you awake? What if you forgot yourself and cried out? What if Comrade Tsang was up and saw me? You know what she's like. It's not a good plan, little miss. And anyway, you can't wake up at four in the morning. It would be bad for your health. You need your sleep."

"Lao Ye, please. I need you to help. If you won't help me, I'm going to be sent home at the end of the year for sure."

"Sent home? Who told you that?"

"Everybody knows one or two girls will fail after the first year, and they'll be sent home," Zhongmei said.

"Ah," said Old Zhou. "That's very cruel, very cruel. Even so, what can I do? I wish I could help, but I don't see how I can."

The two stood and looked at each other for a moment, and then Zhongmei turned to leave. She had thought a lot about Old Zhou since she came up with her plan during her trip home, and now she felt a sharp stab of disappointment at his unwillingness to help.

"Well, never mind," Zhongmei said, her shoulders sagging, her head bowed. "I'll see you later."

"Don't go quite yet," said Old Zhou, stopping Zhongmei at the door. He stroked his chin. His eyes twinkled. "Is your bed next to the window, by any chance?"

"Yes, it is," Zhongmei replied, wondering what that had to do with anything.

"Well, what if there were to be a string dangling down the side of the building?" Old Zhou said. "And what if that string happened to dangle out of the window next to your bed? Naturally I would want to know what that string was doing there, so I'd give it a pull. And if you happened to have tied that piece of string around your wrist, you would feel a tug and wake up—not that waking you up was my intention."

213

"You're a genius, Lao Ye," Zhongmei said, her spirits lifting.

"And it just so happens that I have a length of string right here," said Old Zhou, opening a drawer jumbled with papers, pencils, some tools, and a roll of string. He looked at Zhongmei conspiratorially and whispered, though nobody was nearby. "And here's a little saw." He took a small serrated knife out of the drawer. "You might need this to make a little notch in the windowsill so you can get the string out. Just open the window a crack and hang one end of the string outside. Make sure you push enough of it outside so I can reach it. I'll wake you at four."

"Thank you," Zhongmei said, her eyes welling with tears at finding somebody willing to help her.

"Give a tug back so I'll know you're awake," Old Zhou said.

"I will," said Zhongmei.

"And good luck, little comrade," Old Zhou said.

"Dare to struggle," Zhongmei replied.

Every day now, as she sat in her corner in the fundamentals of ballet class, Zhongmei closely observed what the other girls did. She remembered the movements. She rehearsed them in her head. She imagined herself doing them. And then, while everybody else in the Beijing Dance Academy slept, she practiced them in defiant solitude in studio two. Without fail, Old Zhou pulled on the length of string that always dangled down the brick wall below Zhongmei's window. Every morning, she tugged back, got dressed, rolled the string into a ball and put it in her drawer so nobody would see it, and crept down the stairs, which were empty, silent, and dark. She dashed across the courtyard, moving like a shadow to the main school building, where she flew up the stairs to the second floor, staying as light as she could on her feet as she stole along the corridor, the floorboards nonetheless creaking loudly enough to make her think she would wake up the whole school. But she didn't. Except for Old Zhou in his guardhouse outside, she was probably the only person awake in the entire Dance Academy.

And it was like that every morning in those weeks after Zhongmei's return from the Chinese New Year break. Every morning in fundamentals of ballet she sat in her corner and watched closely as the other girls did their exercises under Teacher Zhu's supervision. She concentrated on every movement and every combination, imagining how she would do them. And then, in the wee hours of the next morning, she made her secret visit to studio two, where she spent two hours doing exactly the drills she wasn't allowed to learn in the very class that had been created to teach them to her, the five positions, the eight basic poses, and the encyclopedia of ballet movements and combinations. She got into the habit of imagining that Teacher Zhu was in the room telling her what to do, almost hearing her voice saying, "*Wu zi bu*"—fifth position—"and leg up, and half turn, that's right, and demi-plié, and on pointe, and grand plié—that's good, and fouetté en tournant to the count of eight—one, two, three, four, five, six, seven, eight, and two, two, three, four, five, six, seven, eight, and three, two, three, four, five, six, seven, eight"—all the way to "eight, two, three, four, five, six, seven, eight." She watched

215

herself in the mirror that lined the studio wall, examining the position of her head, the angle of her arms and hands, the nature of her glance, the curve of her legs, comparing herself to what she had seen in Teacher Zhu's class, and, maybe even more, imitating the pictures that she and Xiaolan looked at every night before going to bed.

On that very first morning, she did the impossible stretching and balancing exercise that had defeated all the girls in Teacher Zhu's class just before the Chinese New Year's break. She lifted her right leg and held it in the crook of her arm; then as she went on pointe on her left foot, she let go of the barre, and she started to topple over right away and had to grab hold again with her left hand to stop her fall. She did it again with the same results, and again, and again, and again, and again, and again. Once she missed her grab at the barre and she did end up spread-eagle on the floor. And she was still trying it, without success, when Old Zhou appeared at the door of studio two.

"It's time to stop," he whispered. "Hurry downstairs."

Zhongmei flew back to her dormitory, gently pushed open the door so it would make no sound, kicked off her ballet slippers, hoisted herself up onto her upper bunk, and crawled under her quilt so when the bell sounded nobody would suspect she hadn't been sleeping all along. She would lie in bed for two or three minutes ardently wishing that she could sleep for hours. But when Old Zhou rang the school bell for the compulsory six o'clock wake-up, she roused herself, stretched, put on her sweats and her weight-loss suit, and went downstairs with the other students for the run in Taoranting Park, the calisthenics and stretching exercises in the courtyard, then fundamentals of ballet, the academic classes, Chinese dance, martial arts, and gymnastics—the whole exhausting day ending with dinner with her leg extended across the table in front of her, evening stretching and practice, and, finally, at nine o'clock, lights-out, face to the wall, sleep. And then, in the pitch blackness of the next morning would come the tug on the string, the misery of being dragged awake like a person yanked by a rope from someplace warm and cozy to someplace cold and inhospitable, and then two more hours of clandestine, solitary self-instruction, undertaken as though learning ballet at a dance academy were some kind of a transgression, a violation of the rules.

22
Lucky

Winter turned to spring, and one Saturday about two months after Zhongmei began her early-morning practice, she went to the cafeteria for lunch to find a scene of commotion. A terrified kitten was in the room, and some boys were gleefully chasing it, throwing aluminum soup spoons at it as it scampered along the walls and between the tables. The kitten was white with orange patches over its frightened eyes. It was meowing in terror and limping on a hind leg. The boys knocked over chairs and slid over tables trying to get to it. The kitten scrambled as best it could behind a door, but now it had no way out, and at that point, Zhongmei, whose tender heart was already bleeding for it, could take no more.

"Stop!" she shouted, and placed herself between the kitten and its pursuers. "You're going to kill it!"

"It's going to die anyway," one of the boys said. "It's a stray. Nobody will feed it. It's better to kill it now and put it out of its misery."

True, it must have been a stray. It must have found an open door or window to get into the building and then followed its nose to the cafeteria. Zhongmei picked it up and held it close. She could feel its heart pounding inside its skinny chest.

"I'll feed it," she said.

"It's dirty," the boy said.

"I'll give it a bath," said Zhongmei, and she ran, the kitten in her arms, back to the dormitory.

Keeping a cat was absolutely forbidden at the Beijing Dance Academy, and Zhongmei knew it. But she already had plans to spend the next day with Policeman Li's family. She would bring the kitten there, and they would take care of it. She knew that they would. But what to do with it in the meantime? She had to hide it for one night. There was no doubt that if Comrade Tsang found out about it, the kitten would be removed from the premises and Zhongmei would be severely reprimanded and required to write an abject self-criticism admitting that she had been selfish, self-centered, and weak, and begging the forgiveness of the school, her teachers, her classmates, and all of China.

But most likely it would be safe in the dormitory. All of the girls would want to protect it. So Zhongmei put the kitten into her dresser drawer. She ran to the cafeteria, ate quickly, and ran back to the dormitory with a steamed bun for the kitten, the kind of food a cat would normally disdain, but not this cat. It was too hungry to be fussy and it devoured the food as though it were a chicken liver or a piece of fish. Then, seeming to know that Zhongmei was trying to save it, it went peacefully back into the dresser drawer and fell asleep so Zhongmei could go off to her afternoon classes.

"It's for your own good," Zhongmei whispered, sliding the drawer shut. "Be quiet. If you make a lot of noise, you'll get us both in trouble."

Zhongmei went impatiently through the afternoon. She did her academic classes, reading, math, and calligraphy, her Chinese classical dance class, acrobatics, and martial arts, thinking always about the kitten. It was when she was practicing her hand and arm movements in classical Chinese dance that she thought of a name for it, Yunqi, which means "lucky" in Chinese. Because lucky it was—saved from death at the hands of the boys, protected by the girls, who would keep its presence a secret. Only one night and a morning, and as long as the kitten didn't go crazy in the drawer, make a lot of noise, and get found out by one of the teachers or security guards or, the worst possibility of all, by Old Maid Tsang, everything would be all right.

When Zhongmei got back to the dormitory, she fed Yunqi another steamed bun. She hid the cat under her sweatshirt and ran down to the laundry room, where she filled a plastic bucket with warm water and some soap and gave Yunqi, who didn't like this aspect of being rescued at all, a bath. Later, she smuggled it out of the dormitory down a narrow path between the building and the compound wall, where Yunqi could do its duty. She brought it back up to the dormitory and made a little nest out of some clothes in her drawer where the kitten could sleep.

"Oh, it's so cute," one of the girls said, and carried Lucky off to another bunk, where some of the other girls began to play with it. For the first time, Lucky started behaving like the kitten it was, despite its limp. It chased after a bit of ribbon that the girls dangled in front of it. Zhongmei, already tired, sat on Xiaolan's bed and the two girls did what they did almost every night, which was look through a book. Soon their attention was riveted by a photograph of a Chinese ballerina doing one of the most difficult steps in the repertoire, a step that Teacher Zhu had told them would only come in their second year of fundamentals of ballet. It was that counterclockwise pirouette, done with the leg raised and the body curved. The dancer in the picture wore a jade-green robe over a flowing white skirt, her hair tied back in a jeweled clasp and hanging down her back. The movement required her to spiral downward until she was almost folded in two and then to spiral back up. The picture showed something magnificent, a true mastery of a movement that required years of practice to get right.

"You shouldn't even look at pictures like that. They'll only make you dream of doing things that you'll never be able to do."

It was Jinhua, of course. Zhongmei and Xiaolan had been so absorbed in the photograph that they hadn't even noticed her peering at the book over their shoulders.

"And you will?" Zhongmei said.

"Oh, sure," Jinhua said. "I did stuff just like that on television in Shanghai when I was just a little girl."

"Like that?" Xiaolan said, pointing at the picture.

"It's hard," said Jinhua, "but look." She took an open space near the entrance to the dorm room, struck a pose, and then whirled into action, her body turning gracefully counterclockwise. She did two good turns, very impressive, but then struggled with her balance on the third turn and had to stop.

"Wooooo-wooo!" Jinhua shouted with delight, ignoring her less-than-perfect ending. A few of the other girls applauded and shouted. Jinhua curtsied and bowed as if to an audience of thousands. She blew kisses. She did a little jeté and turned triumphantly in Zhongmei's direction.

"You shouldn't feel bad," she said. "In Shanghai, we start ballet when we're five years old. It's not your fault that you're so far behind. Anyway, you won't be here much longer. You'll have to go home after you come in dead last in the final performance."

Zhongmei, trying not to pay attention, kept looking at her book.

"Soon you'll be back home, where you can do the rooster dance," Jinhua said, laughing at her own cleverness, and scratching at the floor in imitation of a chicken. A few of the other girls, not all of them, laughed with her.

Zhongmei's ears burned. She looked up at Jinhua, anger flashing in her eyes, but she didn't say anything. She got up, smiled wanly at Xiaolan, and turned to the spot where Jinhua had just done her turn.

"I think the farm girl's gonna try something," Jinhua said.

Zhongmei pretended not to hear. She saw Xiaolan motioning to her, trying to tell her not to do anything. She was afraid it would just open her up to more ridicule. But Zhongmei very calmly took up a position there in the dormitory, and she did what she always did when she needed to perform a difficult movement. She entered into a closed world, the world of a story that she would tell with emotion and movement. She shut out Jinhua and the other silly creatures in the dormitory and concentrated on the story, the story of a girl who stands still, erupts into motion, spirals downward, then upward, and then, after several rotations, returns to motionlessness. It would be the story of a girl who believes at first that something is impossible but, with time, discovers that she can do it.

Dance is like learning to play the piano or another musical instrument. The first stage is learning to hit the notes. It's only after you've learned to do that that you start to make real music, music that moves toward a destination, guided there by the feelings and skill of the musician. You feel the music's motion in your body and your soul. You vary the tone and the tempo; you hit the note sharply and hard or you caress it so that it is soft and lingering. You connect the note before with the note after so that they have a point, tell a story.

That's what Zhongmei did with her Chinese pirouette. She was no longer practicing, she was dancing. She was no longer doing an exercise but was experiencing the joy of art as she strove against gravity, abandoned herself to energy, motion, and perfect balance. That was the difference between her and Jinhua. Jinhua was very skillful technically, but for her, dance was a way of displaying herself, winning admiration, showing off. For Zhongmei it was something beautiful in itself, something to be entered into, lived, and breathed. It could be done in front of an audience, but the dancer could dance when perfectly alone, and the art of it would be just as great.

Zhongmei turned counterclockwise, her right leg steady and strong as a spike buried in the ground, her raised left leg pulling her around, her long, slender body thrown back like a stalk of bamboo swayed by the wind, gracefully curved in the middle. She went once, twice, three times around, spiraling downward on the fourth turn, back up on the fifth and sixth, and coming to a stop on the eighth in exactly the position she was in when she started. She did this not just with more precision and grace than Jinhua had achieved, but with something like ferocity, with a wildness and even a recklessness that had been utterly absent from Jinhua's mechanical reproduction of a schoolgirl's lesson.

The room was quiet as Zhongmei went back to her bed and picked up the book she had been reading. The other girls looked at her.

"Wow!" one of the girls whispered. "We've never seen her do Chinese ballet before. She's good!"

"She's not very good!" Jinhua said desperately, looking around for support. "Her arms and legs were all over the place. It just shows that she doesn't have the background."

"Not very good?" Xiaolan retorted. "She did eight turns. You did two and a half."

"You have to admit, that was pretty amazing," another girl said.

Jinhua's face went red, and she turned angrily away and,

when nobody was paying attention to her, slipped out of the room. Zhongmei could tell that her little unplanned, impromptu performance had changed the other girls' attitudes toward her, and that was good enough for now. If only she could change Teacher Zhu's attitude, everything would be different, but she still didn't know how to do that. Meanwhile, she took a little pleasure in Yunqi, whom she collected from across the room. She held it close, feeling its fragile, furry, and now clean little body and murmuring, "I love you, Yunqi. You brought me luck." She sat on her bed with the kitten in her arms and listened contentedly as it purred.

23

Disaster

Suddenly the door swung open with a bang, and Zhong-mei's brief moment of happiness came crashing to an end. Old Maid Tsang stood red-faced and scowling at the head of the room, the abused door swinging shut behind her. Zhongmei tried to hide Yunqi under her covers, but Comrade Tsang knew exactly what she was looking for and where to find it. She strode swiftly across the room to Zhongmei's bed and snatched up the kitten.

"You know that animals are not allowed," she hissed.

"I know," Zhongmei pleaded, "but I'm taking it to my foster family tomorrow. I'm only keeping it here for one night. It won't do any harm. It's just a little kitten."

"That's against the rules," Comrade Tsang said.

"Please, Comrade Tsang," Zhongmei pleaded. "Can't I keep it, just one night?"

But Comrade Tsang was paying no attention. She was holding Yunqi by the scruff of the neck and swinging her back and

226

forth, up and down, as she shouted in that seemingly amplified voice of hers.

"You selfish, disobedient little brat," she said. Zhongmei had never seen her so furious. "You think the rules are for other people but not for you?"

"You're hurting it!" Zhongmei screamed. "Give it back to me!" She lunged at Tsang to try and pull Yunqi away, but she wasn't quick enough.

"Give her to you?" Tsang shouted, holding the cat out of Zhongmei's reach. She went to a window and yanked it open. Outside was a narrow passageway between the building and the brick wall that went around the entire compound. On the other side of the wall was the busy street.

"Here, take it," Comrade Tsang said, holding Yunqi as if for Zhongmei to take her back. But as Zhongmei reached for her, Tsang raised the kitten over her head and with a windmill motion of her arm hurled it through the open window.

There was a sound of a screech as Yunqi disappeared into the darkness and then there was silence. There was no sound from the ground below. There wasn't a peep from any of the girls in the dormitory, who stood there in a state of shock and disbelief.

Tsang wasn't finished. She whirled around, her red face twisted in fury. "Follow me," she said to Zhongmei, but then, rather than let Zhongmei follow her, she grabbed her by the arm and dragged her out of the room, and Zhongmei, trembling, stricken, horrified, allowed herself passively to be pulled. She remembered as she stumbled out the door that the last person she saw was Jinhua, standing in the corner of the dormitory near the door. She was pale and trembling, and Zhongmei knew instantly: she was the one who had tattled, though she also seemed shocked at the measures Tsang had taken.

Zhongmei and Tsang went downstairs and out of the courtyard.

Am I going to be expelled right away? Zhongmei wondered. She thought that Tsang was going to do the same thing to her that she'd done to Yunqi, kick her out of the school right away and thrust her through the gate and into the night, where she'd have to fend for herself. But she was dragged instead to another building inside the compound where she knew Tsang had her office. She had gone there to ask her for money when she needed something like toothpaste or toilet paper or the bus fare to the Li house.

"Sit down," Tsang told Zhongmei, pointing to a chair. From someplace she produced a single sheet of paper and put it on a desk in front of Zhongmei.

"You will sit there and write a self-criticism," she said. "You will criticize yourself for selfish behavior, putting yourself first, ahead of the Dance Academy and its rules, and you will ask the teachers and staff of the Dance Academy and the Communist Party and the whole Chinese people to forgive you. The sincerity of your self-criticism will determine whether you are able to stay at the school after this infraction."

With that, she turned away, leaving Zhongmei alone in the small room, with a ballpoint pen and a sheet of paper. Zhongmei heard Tsang close the door behind her. Then she heard the sound of a bolt turning and she knew she had been locked into the room from the outside.

Zhongmei could scarcely breathe, she was crying so hard. The tears streamed down her face and fell onto the desk, where she saw them soaking the single piece of paper on which she was supposed to write her self-criticism. She tried to stop crying, feeling that if she couldn't take in some air, she would choke and die. And then she thought the most terrible thought she'd ever thought in her life. She didn't care if she died. It would serve Tsang right. She could have it on her conscience for the rest of her life, assuming she had a conscience. She was hateful. She deserved to die, not Zhongmei, whose terrible crime was to have tried to save a little kitten. Where was the wrong in that? Why had she ever even thought about coming to this cursed school with its cursed people, so sure that everything they did was right when the truth was that what they did was terribly wrong.

Zhongmei banged her hand on the table. She tried to stand up, but as she did so, the light seemed to fade. Her heart felt like it was going to explode. She felt sweat begin to pour out of her. There was a strange high-pitched ringing in her ears, like the sound of the morning bell, only louder, sharper. Her head began to throb and thrum. She felt as if the room was beginning to spin around her, while, miraculously, she stayed motionless. The ringing grew louder, the throbbing more powerful, the spinning accelerated. It seemed as if an icy wind was blowing across her body, and then everything went dark.

24

The Banquet at Hongmen

The next thing she knew, Zhongmei was waking up in a bed with clean sheets. Sunlight was pouring into the room through a curtainless window. Zhongmei looked to one side and saw a row of beds with people lying in them. Bewildered, she turned her head in the other direction and there were Policeman Li and Da-ma standing beside her, a look of concern on their faces.

"You're awake!" Policeman Li said.

"Where am I?" asked Zhongmei.

"You're in the hospital," Policeman Li said.

"The hospital?"

"But you're fine," Policeman Li said. "You got sick. You must have passed out and you were brought here. You slept all night and all morning, and it looks like you needed the rest."

"Oh, my," Zhongmei said, remembering the night before, and how the world was spinning and roaring before she blacked out. "How did I get here?" she asked.

"They found you unconscious and lying on the floor at school, and they brought you here," Policeman Li said. "Early this morning they called the police station to tell me."

Zhongmei remembered the sound of the bolt turning as Comrade Tsang had locked her in the room. The building had been entirely empty at that time of night. Only Tsang knew where Zhongmei was, so it had to have been Tsang who found her and gotten her to the hospital.

"You'll come home with us," Da-ma said, "and get some rest, and after a few days you'll be fine."

"And after that?" Zhongmei asked. "When do I go back to Baoquanling?"

"Baoquanling?" Policeman Li said. "Do you want to go home?"

"No, but I'm being expelled, aren't I?"

"You're not being expelled," Policeman Li said. "You made a mistake, but Comrade Tsang also made a mistake. She reacted too strongly. After you've rested, you'll go back to school."

"I don't want to go back there," Zhongmei said. "I hate everything about that place."

"Well, you'll have some time to think about it. But if you go back, Comrade Tsang will apologize to you. She knows that she treated you too harshly. She should have shown a little sympathy. And after she apologizes to you, you can apologize to her for breaking the rules. It's going to be fine, Zhongmei. Don't worry."

Zhongmei spent two easy weeks at Policeman Li's and

Da-ma's house. Da-ma wouldn't let her do a thing, except eat her favorite dumplings, drink plenty of hot soup, and get plenty of rest. On her last night at "home," the three of them went to the Beijing Opera and saw a performance of *The Banquet at Hongmen*. It's a two-thousand-year-old story based on a real episode from Chinese history in which a powerful, ambitious warlord named Xiang Yu lures his chief rival, a man named Liu Bang, to a supposedly friendly banquet at Hongmen, or Red Gate Palace, with the intention of murdering him. Zhongmei sat breathless for the whole performance. By now she knew the standard devices of Chinese opera. When Xiang Yu, for example, entered the stage wearing a white mask, Zhongmei knew immediately that he was a schemer, full of cunning and deceit, because that's what white represents in Beijing Opera. Liu Bang, who was later to become emperor, wears a red mask. Red means loyalty and virtuousness.

Xiang Yu wore elaborate white robes and a long beard. Accompanied by deafening gongs and cymbals, he walks around the stage for a long time fluttering his hands and fingers at his sides, meaning that he is nervously composing his plot. All sorts of characters make their appearance, including Liu Bang's honorable wife and Xiang Yu's unscrupulous one. There are young, beautiful dancing girls with intricate, colorful headdresses; generals strut the stage in ornate costumes surmounted by curving peacock feathers. Court clowns do amazing acrobatics on the stage. Soldiers streak and bound across the stage, wearing body armor and brandishing broadswords.

In the story, Liu Bang, dressed in long robes of red and black silk brocade, gets advance notice from his spies inside Xiang Yu's camp of the plot to murder him. Still, he goes to the banquet, which gives rise to tense duets between him and Xiang Yu. The audience in the drafty Beijing Opera theater is in a state of suspense. Will Liu Bang react to the plot in time, or will he be killed? Just as Xiang Yu's henchmen are about to slit Liu Bang's throat, loyal guards burst into the hall, and a climactic battle takes place involving slashing swords and spears, acrobatic kicks, whirling jumps and somersaults, all of it precisely choreographed and timed so the stage is transformed into an elaborate panorama of moving parts.

When Zhongmei got home that night, she thought about the story of Xiang Yu and Liu Bang, and how, in a way, it reflected her own story. She was like Liu Bang, loyal and honest. One of the Chinese characters in her given name, Zhong, means "loyal, faithful, honest." Unsuspecting, she had been lured to a sort of Hongmen Palace—in her case, the Beijing Dance Academy—only to be betrayed there by a tricky and powerful enemy, a sort of Xiang Yu, or maybe Xiang Yu's treacherous wife. She imagined herself in an audience watching her own drama, murmuring with excitement, asking the question: Would she, like Liu Bang, be able to survive this dastardly attack and turn the tables on her enemy?

Policeman Li had told her not to worry; everything would be fine. But she wasn't sure. The episode with the kitten had earned her a new adversary, Comrade Tsang, adding to the adversary she already had, Teacher Zhu. When she got back to school, she was supposed to apologize to Comrade Tsang, a distasteful duty if ever there was one, but Zhongmei would do it. She couldn't afford to have both Teacher Zhu and Comrade Tsang against her, or Zhongmei's own *Banquet at Hongmen* would not have a happy ending.

25
Caught!

*P*oliceman Li brought her to school on the back of his motorcycle the next afternoon, Sunday. Zhongmei ran up to the dormitory, where most of the girls greeted her warmly, even Jinhua, who seemed both sheepish and friendly. Xiaolan threw her arm over Zhongmei's shoulder, and the two of them marched off to the cafeteria for the evening meal. Zhongmei wasted no time in telling her only true friend everything that had happened, from the moment Old Maid Tsang dragged her out of the dormitory to her waking up in the hospital and the two weeks she had spent with Policeman Li's family.

"Things are going to go better," Xiaolan told her. "I'm sure they're going to treat you differently from now on."

Zhongmei hoped so. But first there was the not very enticing matter of the meeting with Comrade Tsang that she needed to take care of. Policeman Li had told her to do that as soon as she got back to school.

"Tell her you realize that you should have asked her

permission to keep the cat for one night," he had told Zhong-mei. "She'll accept your apology and then she'll apologize for the way she treated you, and the way she treated the cat. That way everybody will say they're sorry and will save face at the same time."

That night, Zhongmei went across the courtyard to Tsang's office and knocked on the door. "Come in," she heard Comrade Tsang say, and so nervous she was short of breath, she pushed open the door. Tsang was sitting with her back to the office entrance, and as Zhongmei stood behind her, she noted how thick her neck was and how severely her hair was cut.

Zhongmei cleared her throat to announce her presence. Comrade Tsang turned around and did something that Zhong-mei had never seen her do before. She smiled.

"I've come to say I'm sorry for breaking the rules," Zhong-mei started, encouraged by the look on Comrade Tsang's face. She had practiced what she was going to say as if it were a performance that she was going to do in front of an audience.

"I know it was wrong of me," she said. "I ask you to forgive me for my bad behavior. I've learned my lesson and I'll never do anything like that again."

Comrade Tsang looked at her, and Zhongmei felt she saw a softening in her eyes.

"You know," Comrade Tsang said. "It's not easy to be in charge of almost one hundred and fifty students. That's how many we have here, counting all the grades. Rules are for a purpose. We have to maintain order, so everybody can do their work, and maintaining order happens to be my job."

She fell silent as if waiting for Zhongmei to agree.

"Yes," Zhongmei said. "It's a very important responsibility."

"But there's also room for understanding and for kindness," Comrade Tsang said, "and I'm sorry I didn't show you any of that on the night in question. That was my mistake."

Zhongmei looked down, glad, but not knowing what to say.

"You don't know what to say," Comrade Tsang said. "That's all right. I wouldn't know quite what to say either if I were in your shoes. Let's leave it at that. Thank you for coming. Let's consider this matter settled."

Comrade Tsang smiled again, and then, a bit awkwardly, she turned back to her desk. Zhongmei backed out of her office and into the courtyard outside, feeling as if a great burden had been lifted from her shoulders. She had done it. She had apologized. And Comrade Tsang had even apologized to her! She was human after all!

The next morning very early, Zhongmei got up by herself, without Old Zhou pulling on the string outside her window. After her absence of two weeks, she hadn't told him to start waking her up again. She didn't even know what time it was, only that she had been sleeping for quite a while, that it was still pitch dark, and that she had to resume her secret practice sessions. She climbed stealthily down from her upper bunk, got dressed, pulled on her ballet slippers, and stole across the courtyard to studio two.

After leaving Comrade Tsang's office the previous night, Zhongmei had felt a mix of emotions. Relief was the main one, relief that the exchange of apologies was over and seemed to have gone well. She felt that Tsang wasn't her enemy anymore. Still, nothing had changed with Teacher Zhu, and Zhongmei's feeling of relief quickly turned to a sort of dread when she thought about the ballet class she most likely wouldn't be allowed to take that morning. Then she thought about the portrait of Chairman Mao in her home at Baoquanling and how it was telling her to dare to struggle, dare to win. She remembered Zhongqin's words of encouragement, how she had told her to do her best and not give up, and with those memories, Zhongmei's fear turned into resolve, and resolve turned into a plan.

"I'm not going to just go to my corner and sit there," Zhongmei told Xiaolan the night before, after she got back to the dormitory. "I'm going to stay at the barre no matter what."

"Oh, I don't know if you should do that," Xiaolan said.

"Why not?" Zhongmei replied. "What can she do to me?"

"She could accuse you of disobeying her. She could cause you lots of trouble."

"More trouble than she causes me already?"

"Well, you have a point," Xiaolan said, seeing the brilliance of Zhongmei's plan. If Teacher Zhu complained to the higher-ups about Zhongmei's behavior, she would have to explain why she hadn't allowed her to take fundamentals of ballet, and she probably didn't want the higher-ups to know about that.

And so, there she was again after her two-week absence, determined to practice especially hard, because this wasn't going to be an ordinary day. She went through her motions looking at herself in the mirror—first position, and demi-plié, fifth position, grand plié, and one, two, three, four, five, six, seven, eight, and two, two, three, four, five, six, seven, eight, and three, two, three, four, five, six, seven, eight. . . . Zhongmei moved on to a combination, giving herself instructions: first, adagio, slow . . . plié, développé, battement tendu. Then she moved to a fouetté en tournant, her right toe touching her left knee, her left knee bending, a pirouette, and then again— slowly at first, then moving to allegro, a faster motion, one, two, three, four, five, six, seven, eight, and two, two, three, four, five, six, seven . . .

There was a sound. It was a creaking noise, like footsteps on old wood. Zhongmei froze in mid-pirouette, staring at the studio door. Probably just the sound of an old building, she said to herself. She didn't know exactly what time it was, but certainly nobody would be up now, besides herself and Old Zhou. The creaking got louder and closer. The studio door had a glass window that acted as a mirror, and terror gripped Zhongmei as the reflection began to change. Zhongmei saw a corner of the empty room reflected in the wobbly glass, then a darkened window above the ballet barre, then she herself standing a little farther along on the barre. The door was swinging open, and Zhongmei's heart pounded wildly as Jia Zuoguang strode into the room.

He looked very large, a giant. He seemed to fill the entire studio. Zhongmei felt that he was close to her and towering over her even though in truth he was standing quite far away.

"*Xiao mei zi*," he said—young girl. He pronounced the

words in that fashion of adults when they are about to issue a reprimand. "What on earth are you doing?"

"Um . . . I'm practicing," Zhongmei replied.

"Don't you know that to be out of your room at this hour is against the rules," Vice Director Jia said. "In fact, it's a very serious infraction of the rules. You know that, of course."

"Yes," Zhongmei said meekly. "I know it."

"I see that you are practicing," Jia said, "but there is a time for practice and a time for rest, and now is the time for rest."

Zhongmei stared at the floor horrified at what was happening. She was there in studio two in order to avoid being expelled from school, and now she was going to be expelled anyway, for trying too hard not to be.

"Only the other day you broke the rule against keeping an animal in the school," Jia said. "And now you're breaking another rule. This is very serious."

Zhongmei didn't know what to say.

"It's a great privilege to study at this school," Jia said. "It's a gift given to you by the people of China, and you think you can do whatever you want?"

Zhongmei stared at the floor.

"Well, answer me. Do you think the rules and regulations weren't meant for you?"

"No," Zhongmei said. "But—"

"But nothing," Jia interrupted. "Go to your dormitory and back to bed immediately. We'll decide what to do about this later."

"Yes, sir," Zhongmei replied, and she walked past him to

the door. Her heart ached. She had ruined everything now. Now she would surely have to go back to Baoquanling in defeat, and she would have to go back right away. She wouldn't even be able to wait until the end of the school year.

But then she thought, Wait a minute. If I don't learn on my own what the others are learning in fundamentals of ballet, I'll fail the exams anyway, and they'll send me home. No matter what I do, the outcome will be the same. And I'm doing nothing wrong. It's like Yunqi. I broke a rule, but the rule was wrong. It shouldn't be against the rules to save a kitten, and it shouldn't be against the rules to practice on my own if my teacher doesn't allow me to practice in class.

Zhongmei turned around and walked back to the ballet barre under one of the dark windows of studio two.

"I'm sorry, Vice Director Jia, but I don't want to go back to bed," she said.

"What!" Vice Director Jia said, incredulous. "Didn't you hear what I told you to do?"

It would be hard to exaggerate how terrified Zhongmei felt, but once more she held her ground.

"I know it's against the rules to be up at night," she said. "But it's the only thing I can do."

"Explain yourself," Vice Director Jia said. "What does that mean, it's the only thing you can do?" He still looked stern, but Zhongmei detected a slight lessening of his anger, just a hint of kindness. "You have a full program of classes. Now you need your rest. You can ruin your health this way. The rules we have are for a purpose. They're for your own good."

"I have to do this," Zhongmei said quietly.

"Why, may I ask?" Jia said, and like that day, which seemed eons ago, when he had given her a second chance at the audition improvisation, Zhongmei detected a shift from strictness to sympathy, or at least curiosity.

"Because I'm slower than the other girls," Zhongmei said. "I'm not as pretty or as graceful as they are, and I need extra practice to catch up. Or else I'm going to be sent home."

"First of all, I remember you from the audition, and you're not a bit less pretty or graceful than the other girls," Jia said, and Zhongmei's heart took a hesitant leap at those words. Was this just flattery or was it true? "Second," Jia continued, "you have the same classes as everybody else. If you need some special help, surely your teachers will give it to you."

With that, Zhongmei couldn't help but give a rueful little chuckle.

"You don't know what . . . That's just . . . No," Zhongmei said. "I don't get special help. I don't get any help at all. I'm not even allowed to take the most important class in this school! And you think I can get extra help?"

And with that, in a great outpouring of words and tears, Zhongmei explained to China's most famous dancer how she had spent the whole school year so far having to sit in a corner in Teacher Zhu's class, and how Teacher Zhu had ridiculed her when she had made her audition for her class, and how none of the rehearsal teachers would take her for their classes either. She told Vice Director Jia that Teacher Zhu and the other girls were saying that she would be sent home for good at the end of the year, and that's why she was breaking the rule against being out of bed before the six o'clock wake-up bell.

Jia listened in silence. He didn't interrupt, and he didn't seem angry anymore. But when she finished, he told her, "Nonetheless, rules are rules and are not to be broken. This is something you should have spoken to me about a long time ago, and now that you've taken matters into your own hands, I'm not sure what I can do for you."

"Am I going to be expelled?" Zhongmei asked. Her voice was quiet.

"If you were the vice director of this school and a girl violated the rules like you have done, twice in two weeks, what would you do?" he asked.

"I . . ." Zhongmei hesitated. A long silence filled the room. "I don't know," she said at last. "No, I do know. I would praise her for trying hard. I wouldn't expel her."

She thought she saw the beginnings of a smile on Jia's face, but he nonetheless said, "If one girl can break the rules, then all the girls can break the rules, and then there will be no order at all."

"Yes," Zhongmei said, her head down. "I guess I'll go back to bed."

"What move were you practicing just now when I came in?" Jia asked.

"What move?" she said. "Can I show you?"

"No, this is not the time."

"When can I show you, then?"

"I don't know, I'm quite . . ." Jia began before trailing off. "OK," he resumed. "Let's see it."

Zhongmei turned and went back to the barre. At first she was terribly nervous and a little bit shaky, but then she began to concentrate. She felt the movements inside of her as if the muscles of her arms and legs acted on their own. She didn't forget that Jia was standing there, and yet she danced for herself, picking up the tempo, her movements becoming bolder, her leaps and kicks higher, her arabesques steeper, her fouettés en tournant faster; she did pirouettes in the Chinese fashion, counterclockwise, her body arching and following her raised left foot, spinning and spiraling herself into a crouch on the floor and then unfolding, coming up gradually, spinning, spinning, faster and faster, her body arched backward, one arm thrown over her head, the other trailing in front of her. She danced as if that was what she was born to do, and she knew that she was.

At last she stopped. She looked to where she thought Jia was standing, but the room was empty, almost as if her entire encounter with him had been a dream. Zhongmei stood there with her mouth agape. Had she imagined this entire incident? She spun around thinking that perhaps Vice Director Jia was behind her, but there was only the barre, and behind the barre the mirror in which she saw herself reflected, a small skinny girl in the gray of the earliest dawn, alone and yet full of desire and hope and confusion.

Suddenly Old Zhou appeared at the door.

"I saw the light on," he said. "I thought it must be you. It's time to go back to the dormitory. Hurry!"

Zhongmei flew down the stairs, into the courtyard, up the stairs, and into her bed just in time to hear the wake-up bell. She lay there for a minute, wishing that she could sleep, maybe have a beautiful dream in which the Beijing Dance Academy was a friendly, cozy place where she was happy. She climbed down from her upper bunk and went to her drawer to put on her sweat suit and its plastic covering for early-morning exercise. The day was starting like any other, and she didn't know if she was now going to be expelled from the Beijing Dance Academy because of her continued bad behavior, or if she had saved herself by dancing more beautifully than any other girl Vice Director Jia had ever observed.

26
The Progress Prize

The exercises done, Zhongmei went with Xiaolan for breakfast. She watched as the other girls checked their names on the rehearsal lists for that afternoon, something that Zhongmei didn't bother to do anymore because she knew her name wouldn't be there.

"Zhongmei," Xiaolan said. "You'd better look at this."

Zhongmei looked up at the bulletin board. There was the usual list of rehearsal teachers, a studio number, and the names of the boys and girls chosen for that rehearsal. But there was something else that Zhongmei couldn't quite believe was really there. Her name, written in conspicuously large characters, as if the person who wrote them wanted to be sure they were seen by everybody, was there also, for the first time ever! And the name of the rehearsal teacher just above it was somebody who never taught rehearsal. It was Jia Zuoguang! And the dance she was to do: *Butterfly Lovers* duet!

This was amazing. Zhongmei had been chosen by the

biggest star of the Beijing Dance Academy to rehearse a duet from *Butterfly Lovers*! It was one of the most famous and difficult dances in the Chinese classical repertory, a drama about a girl who, in order to become a scholar, pretends to be a boy. First-year students did some simple duets, which they practiced at rehearsal, but not *Butterfly Lovers*, which was technically very difficult, involving all sorts of complicated lifts and acrobatic movements. And since no boy was listed on Jia Zuoguang's rehearsal notice, it appeared as though Zhongmei's partner would be none other than Vice Director Jia himself! Zhongmei could hear a kind of oohing and aahing around her as the other students, boys and girls, absorbed the remarkable information on the bulletin board. She heard her name whispered with surprise and the words *"Butterfly Lovers"* and "Jia Zuoguang" spoken with reverence. The girl nobody wanted and that everybody knew was going to be returned home at the end of the year had suddenly been chosen for something very special. What could be going on?

Zhongmei went through the morning in a kind of trance. She hardly noticed when Teacher Zhu treated her like any other girl in fundamentals of ballet, letting her take her place at the barre and giving her the same rough treatment she meted out to everybody. Later, she attended calligraphy, math, and reading classes, barely paying attention. She had lunch standing up in the cafeteria, her leg stretched across the table in front of her, unaware of what she was eating. She didn't sleep a wink at nap time. The time for rehearsal came and she stood at the bulletin board, because no studio had been listed for her solo with Jia. All the other students disappeared to their assignments. Zhongmei waited by herself, and just as she was beginning to wonder if this too was something she had imagined, Jia Zuoguang appeared down the corridor, a smile on his handsome face.

"Hello, *xiao mei zi*," he said. "Come with me," and he led Zhongmei up the stairs to the third-floor studios. "Listen," he told her. "I don't have time to practice with you myself, but I'm going to put you in Teacher Peng Guimin's solo class. It's for second-year students, but I'm sure you can handle it."

He opened the door to a studio, and Zhongmei saw half a dozen girls and Teacher Peng.

"Xiao Peng," Jia said, using the diminutive for Teacher Peng. "This is Li Zhongmei. Do me a favor and take her in your class."

"Well, I guess I can take her for today," Teacher Peng said.

"No, I want you to take her for the rest of the year," Jia said, "and prepare her for her final-day performance."

"But I already have a full complement," the surprised Teacher Peng protested. "And she's just a first-year student, I think. This class is for—"

"Yes, I know," Jia interrupted. "Never mind that. Please just take her. You'd be doing me an enormous favor. I'll explain the situation to you later. Meanwhile, do your best with her. You'll see that she's a very hard worker and very talented. Do what you can with her, and I want to see progress by the end of the semester."

"Yes, of course, Zuoguang," Teacher Peng said. Turning to

Zhongmei, she said, "Take a spot there, and just follow as best you can. My schedule is full and I don't have time to give you any extra attention, but come every day and we'll see what you can do."

Zhongmei took a place in the back row, feeling out of place among all these older girls, but thrilled as well.

"We're doing the solo parts of the Dunhuang dance," Teacher Peng said for Zhongmei's benefit. "You've heard of Dunhuang probably?"

Zhongmei nodded, but in truth she wasn't sure. Anyway she understood that she wasn't doing *Butterfly Lovers*. Jia had just written that down to impress everybody else. But what was important was that he wanted her to do well at her final performance, and he was giving her a special chance to succeed.

"One of our most famous Chinese places is called Dunhuang," Teacher Peng explained. "It's in Gansu Province in western China. More than a thousand years ago, Buddhist monks painted the walls of caves there. The Dunhuang dance is based on one of those paintings. It shows a goddess, called a flying apsara, who spreads the wisdom of the Buddha across the universe. Just try to follow."

Zhongmei did. And she did the next day as well, learning the intricate movements and poses of the flying apsaras, who were a kind of nymph flying through the air trailing long, curling gossamer ribbons. On Zhongmei's second day of rehearsal, the girls spent the entire time on a single movement, a very hard one. The dancer stands with one arm raised over her head, the other extended in front of her, the body arched backward, one foot raised behind her while she turns smoothly through one or more complete rotations on the other.

"The trick is to hold the position and to turn in a single, smooth, slow motion," Teacher Peng said. "Don't turn a little bit, then stop, then turn a bit more. You have to get enough momentum to complete the turn at the same speed all the way around, but not so much momentum that you start fast and end up slow, or go too far around so you end up with your behind facing the audience."

The other girls laughed at that, but Zhongmei was thinking. The same speed all the way around! One smooth uninterrupted motion! Zhongmei wondered if she could ever do that. After a while of trying, her hip and calf muscles burned with the effort, but she kept on trying.

"Not too fast," Teacher Peng said. "Slowly. It's even harder when done slowly, but it's more graceful and stately that way."

At the end of the class each of the girls did the movement in turn while the other girls watched. Most of them could manage at least one respectable turn, but when Zhongmei's turn came, she failed miserably, flailing her arms to keep her balance while wobbling on her right foot as she tried to make the turn.

"Don't be discouraged," Teacher Peng said. "Nobody gets it on the first try. We'll do it again tomorrow."

That night, during the practice hour before lights-out, Zhongmei went into a corner of studio two and practiced it over and over. She felt it was like a figure skater's spin, except a figure skater has a metal blade and ice to turn on. A dancer has only the ball of her foot, which had to be planted firmly in the ground like a spike and to be able to turn effortlessly at the same time. Zhongmei took up the position, her arm over her head like an overhanging branch, her leg curved backward, her body tilted, and then turned. And again. And again. By the end of the hour, she was able to do one turn well enough so she didn't look like a clown pretending to be a dancer. The next day, she tried again and the day after that, until one turn looked pretty good to her as she examined herself in the mirror, but the second and third turns were wobbly and uneven. Would she ever get it?

Zhongmei also went to rehearsal every afternoon, and she kept on practicing at night. After two weeks, Teacher Peng had each of the students in her class do a small performance, just that movement, in front of the others.

"Those of you who have mastered it will go on to the next movement; those of you who haven't will prepare something a bit easier for the final performance," she said.

Zhongmei, as the youngest in the class, was the last to go. She watched as the other girls did the movement, and all of them were pretty good. They could all do at least one excellent turn, some of them two and even three. After each mini-performance, all the girls applauded politely, wanting, no doubt, to be applauded in turn.

It was Zhongmei's turn. She could see from the expressions on the other girls' faces that not much was expected of her. She was, after all, only a first-year student, and she had started the rehearsal late, so surely she would be behind the others. If she managed one shaky turn, she would be doing pretty well. As long as she made it all the way around, stopped with her front toward the audience, and didn't end up sprawled on the studio floor.

She took her place in the middle of the studio. She saw herself in the mirror on the opposite wall as she raised her arms and went into her spin. When she finished, the girls, sitting on the floor in front of the mirror, were silent and expressionless. There was no applause at all. Zhongmei was crestfallen. She felt she had done pretty well. Why this disapproving silence from her fellow students? Did they hate her because she was a farm girl, or because she was just a first-year student who had gotten special treatment from Vice Director Jia?

Then, after a long minute, one of the girls started to clap her hands. And then the others joined in, not perfunctorily like before, but loud and long. Zhongmei saw that Teacher Peng, who was standing on the side, was also applauding and smiling as she did so.

"Three perfect rotations!" she exclaimed when the applause had finally died away. "And two weeks ago, you could hardly do one! I think at the very least, Zhongmei deserves the prize for most progress."

It wasn't lost on Zhongmei that Teacher Peng wanted her to succeed, in contrast to Teacher Zhu, who wanted her to fail, and that Teacher Peng would view a success by Zhongmei as a success for herself. This realization brought tears to Zhongmei's eyes.

"The next step is the long sleeves," Teacher Peng said as she handed Zhongmei a ribbon of blue-gray silk. The two of them were alone in the rehearsal studio, because Teacher Peng had been so pleased with Zhongmei's progress that she was giving her extra classes to prepare for the final-day performance. The ribbon was divided in the middle by a heavy twist of fabric that rested on the dancer's shoulders, so that the lengths on each side were thirty-five feet long.

"They're awfully long," Zhongmei said. "How can anybody possibly control them?"

"They're long because they symbolize streaks of heavenly light, and I'm going to teach you how to control them."

Teacher Peng placed the twist of fabric over Zhongmei's shoulders and put one ribbon end in each of Zhongmei's hands.

"The idea is to think the ribbons into the air, to think them into swirling around you like the breeze, and when you have your thoughts right, your arms and hands will take care of the rest."

"OK, I'm thinking, but the ribbons aren't flying," Zhongmei said, and the two of them laughed.

"Think the ribbon into the air, and as you think, raise your arms and begin to turn to give them some lift."

Zhongmei followed directions.

"That's right," Teacher Peng said. "They're both airborne. Now keep thinking them up in the air. Keep turning. And then, whirl your right arm over your head so the right ribbon arches up; then just as it begins to settle down, do the same thing with the left one."

Zhongmei whirled the right ribbon, but it caught on the left-hand ribbon, and the whole thing ended up in a tangled heap on the floor.

"That's OK," Teacher Peng called. "It would have been a

miracle if you'd done it the first time. Try again. Think the ribbon up. Think it swirling around your head. Think it describing circles in front of you. And then your hands and arms will do what's necessary."

"I have two weeks to get ready," Zhongmei said. "Do you really think I can do it?"

"My dear," said Teacher Peng, "I think you can do anything you set your mind to."

And for the first time in the nine months that Zhongmei had been at the Beijing Dance Academy, she felt something like happiness.

27
Triumph

"*M*ay I speak with you?"

Zhongmei, lying on her upper bunk just before lights-out, was so absorbed in the book she was reading that at first she didn't even hear Jinhua's voice. The book contained a collection of reproductions of the Dunhuang cave paintings that she studied every night, pictures that teemed with life, with amazing, sinuous images, a lustrous blending of pastels, and costumes of intricate elegance. Being extremely old, many of the paintings were faded and cracked, but that only increased their appeal for Zhongmei. There was a burnished quality about them, a radiance that came from within that something brand-new and shiny could never have. Here, for example, was a celestial musician floating in a space of streaming colors exactly like the long silk ribbons kept aloft by the apsara Zhongmei incarnated in the dance she was learning, her body curved gracefully, her long, slender fingers cradling a flute. It was as though the image were speaking across the

255

centuries to Zhongmei, telling her, "Be beautiful and ethereal like me; bring me to life."

"May I speak with you, please?"

The voice was shy, a bit hesitant, and Zhongmei looked up to see Jinhua standing in front of her upper bunk, looking uncharacteristically nervous.

"I'm sorry about the kitten," she blurted out.

In the weeks after Zhongmei's return from the hospital, she and Jinhua had never spoken, but Zhongmei noticed a change in her, and ever since Zhongmei had been chosen for the Dunhuang solo rehearsal, Jinhua seemed to look at her with respectfulness in her eyes. The mockery of before was gone.

"I'm afraid of cats," she told Zhongmei. "And I told Old Maid Tsang that you had one. But I never thought she'd do that," and she made a movement with her arm. "I'm really sorry."

"It's OK," Zhongmei said. "It was Comrade Tsang who threw the cat out the window, not you."

"Also," Jinhua said, her eyes moist, "I'm sorry for making fun of you."

Zhongmei shrugged. She didn't know what to say. She didn't want to forgive Jinhua exactly, but she was glad that the girl was trying to make amends.

"It's nothing," she finally said.

"Everybody can't wait to see you perform the Dunhuang solo," Jinhua said, and she shyly turned away. "I know you're going to be great."

"I hope so," Zhongmei said. "The final's only a week away, and I'm kind of nervous."

"Don't be nervous," Jinhua said. "Everybody was wrong about you. I was wrong about you. Everybody thought a girl from the country couldn't be a great dancer. But you are going to be a great dancer. You're going to be the best one."

The final came in June on the last day of classes, and, as it happened, on Zhongmei's twelfth birthday, June 27. Every year all the students performed the dances they had been studying in rehearsal for all the other students and the teachers, plus an assortment of government officials and family members, who sat in the small Dance Academy Theater next to the cafeteria. The seats were curved and upholstered, like in a real theater. There was a real stage, framed in red velvet curtains.

All seven of the girls in Teacher Peng's Dunhuang solo class were going to perform, one after the other, and Teacher Peng told Zhongmei that she would go last.

The day before, she'd taken Zhongmei to her office and fitted her with shimmering silk pantaloons, a light turquoise blouse, and pale blue slippers whose toes pointed up. It was the first time ever that Zhongmei had worn a costume, and it felt miraculously cool and sleek on her skin.

On the day of the final, Teacher Peng again brought Zhongmei to her office and applied makeup—another first for Zhongmei. She highlighted her eyebrows, powdered her cheeks, painted her lips a luscious red, applied mascara to her lower eyelashes and more heavily on the upper ones. She wound a portion of Zhongmei's hair, which had grown long during her year at the Beijing Dance Academy, in a kind of turban around her head while leaving a thick, luxuriant strand to cascade down the middle of her back. She used long gold-colored pins to attach a glittering, bejeweled hair ornament, and then she told Zhongmei to look at herself in the mirror.

"You think you're the ugly farm girl," she said. "Look at yourself."

Zhongmei looked. She saw her oval face, her high cheekbones, her full red lips. She saw her crescent eyebrows, her peach-colored translucent skin no longer blotched and ruddy from the Baoquanling climate, her long, slender neck, and her dark fiery eyes. She remembered the frightened, uncertain country girl who had appeared at the audition a year earlier, and she realized that she was still that girl, but she was somebody else at the same time, somebody different. There was still the eagerness in her eyes, though a touch of sadness had been added, and maybe also a bit of wisdom. But the radiant creature looking back at her in Teacher Peng's wood-framed mirror was somebody she scarcely knew existed. Most of all, she noted that she could be elegant and . . . what was the word that Teacher Zhu had used to describe what she lacked? *Refined*. She had been told she lacked refinement. Now here was the proof that that judgment was wrong. The girl in the mirror was refinement itself.

Zhongmei put down the mirror.

"Do you think, if I do well today, that I'll be allowed back at school next year?" she asked.

"Allowed back? Oh, of course," Teacher Peng exclaimed. "We're never going to let you get away."

Standing in the wings waiting for her entrance with the

258

other girls who had learned the Dunhuang solo, Zhongmei could hear the murmur of the audience. Teacher Peng had gone in ahead of her, having given the order of appearance to each of the performers. Zhongmei watched as each of the girls crossed from the shadows of the wings into the bright light of the stage and did her performance. Each of them was costumed similarly to Zhongmei, but not exactly the same. Each of them seemed to Zhongmei radiant, lovely, and accomplished, and she prayed that the audience would accept her as one of them. There was polite applause for each of the six girls who preceded her. Each girl, as she returned to the wings, gave the long ribbon to the girl who was to follow her onto the stage.

She heard a voice over the loudspeaker: "Our next and last performer, Li Zhongmei." The last of the second-year girls to perform placed the ribbon over Zhongmei's shoulders, and Zhongmei walked onto the stage with the delicate steps that she'd practiced, the steps that made her seem to be gliding above the floor, floating in the ether. She made a half circle, the long ribbon trailing behind her, her tiara pulling at her hair, her heart pounding, beads of nervous sweat forming on her upper lip, tempting her to lick them off, though she knew better than to do that.

Zhongmei stopped at stage center. The music started. She began her first series of movements, slow and supple like an adagio, dignified and delicate, but also acrobatic, and she knew that she would be all right. She shut out the theater, and the audience, and even Jia Zuoguang, whom she had seen when she first came into the theater, sitting in the middle of the front row. She forgot about her terror of being the clumsy, clunky girl from the countryside without the refinement required for ballet. She entered into a state of something like serenity. She smiled a gentle smile. She dwelled in a closed world where there was only the sky, the wisps of cloud, and the movements of the goddess who incarnated both wisdom and loveliness. Her long ribbons at first described simple circles in front of her and over her head, but as they whirled faster and faster, Zhongmei thinking them into place, they became ovals within ovals and circles within circles, as though Zhongmei commanded the elegant and powerful forces of nature around her. She glided across the floor as if propelled by some magical force. She leaped high, one foot arching back and almost touching the nape of her neck, the other flung up and forward to the level of her face. She came to a stop, raised her arms behind her, and lifted her leg in front of her and across her body, looking exactly like one of the paintings she had studied before going to bed at night, and then, her foot gripping the floor, keeping her body in absolute wobble-free balance, she straightened her leg and extended it upward, holding that tableau for a gravity-defying span, and then she swept low with her upper body, her arms raised like wings, the ribbons like fountains of colors draping her on either side, her leg curved behind and turned in the deliberate continuous motion she had rehearsed for hours and hours, days and weeks until she had gotten it right.

The dance was the most intense three minutes of Zhongmei's life, and when it was over, it took her a few moments to realize that her performance was being greeted by loud applause and whistles. She curtsied, her arms crossed in front of her. The boys in the back rows were banging their feet on the floor, clapping with hands held over their heads. Zhongmei looked at Teacher Peng, who smiled back at her and nodded her head up and down. Xiaolan was smiling at her and giving her the thumbs-up. Zhongmei saw Jinhua and noticed that tears were streaking her face, whether tears of happiness, tears of remorse, or tears of envy, Zhongmei couldn't tell. She noticed that Teacher Zhu wasn't smiling, but she applauded dutifully and correctly. She saw Old Maid Tsang, who clapped and smiled as if she had been Zhongmei's biggest supporter all along. Seeing her, an image of Yunqi flashed across the screen of her mind and a dollop of sadness mingled with her joy. Zhongmei's eyes met those of Vice Director Jia, who could have punished her after he caught her in the studio that day a couple of months before but decided to understand her instead. He had given her a chance, and by the look on his face, she had met his expectations. Zhongmei bowed her head to him and smiled.

Then it was over. There were the sounds of the audience as they got up from their seats. A couple of men in well-tailored Mao suits came backstage and shook Zhongmei's hand. They told her they represented the Ministry of Culture. "You are like a swan," one of them said, and Zhongmei murmured a polite thank-you. Through the wings, she could see that Jia Zuoguang had taken a place at the front of the theater and was wishing everybody a good summer vacation, telling everybody to keep in shape and be ready for more hard work the next year. Teacher Peng hugged Zhongmei and told her that she was proud of how well she had done.

It was all happening so quickly that Zhongmei was only barely able to focus on the enormous meaning of this short performance for her. She had made it! The farm girl who had been asked to instruct the others in the sound of a rooster, who had had to sit in a corner of a room denied the chance to do the very thing she had come all the way to Beijing to do, the frightened bumpkin who had been expelled from class when she didn't know what it meant to go on television, had proved Teacher Zhu wrong. She could put her worries aside. She would come back next year. She would be a dancer. She thought about her grandmother and her parents, her brothers and sisters. She must write to her *da-jie* right away and tell her the good news.

"Didn't I tell you a long time ago that you were the best of us all?" came a familiar voice behind her.

Zhongmei turned around and threw her arms around the tall, beautiful girl who alone had wanted to be her friend in the midst of her loneliness.

"Oh, Little Orchid," Faithful Plum said. "I'm not the best. You're much better than me."

"The year began pretty badly, but it ended well, didn't it?" Xiaolan said. "That's because you never gave up. I admire you for that. I think you're great."

"I almost gave up," Zhongmei said. "If it hadn't been for you, I would have crumbled into dust. I would have died, and they would have carried me out of here on a donkey cart."

"Well, now they're going to carry you out of here in a limousine," Xiaolan said.

The two girls, twelve years old now, hugged and wept.

"You're going to be a star," Xiaolan said, sniffling.

"We'll both be stars," Zhongmei replied, her cheeks wet, her eyes glistening, her mascara running, her makeup streaked.

"We'll travel to America," Xiaolan said. "Maybe, someday."

"We'll jump on televisions together!" Zhongmei exclaimed. "Right on top!"

And both girls laughed through their tears.

Epilogue

*Z*hongmei did go to America, and so did Xiaolan. The two of them performed at the Joyce Theater in New York City and many other places in the United States from Boston to Los Angeles, and her signature number, the solo that never failed to win the acclaim of audiences and critics alike, was the very one she did in her final-day performance at the end of her first year at the Beijing Dance Academy, *Flying Apsaras*. But America was later. First, Zhongmei, at the age of eighteen, graduated from the Beijing Dance Academy. She spent two more years doing advanced study at the Dance Academy and then seven years as a principal dancer for the leading Chinese dance troupe, traveling to almost every country in Asia to perform. Along the way, she won the most prestigious and hotly contested dance competitions in China.

And she went on television too. She performed every year during the special New Year's Eve broadcast that is watched by just about every person in China, all 1.3 billion of them. She was famous, recognized by people on the street, asked for her autograph. Meanwhile, the story of her first difficult year became legend at the Beijing Dance Academy, its main episodes passed on from the older students to the younger ones, so that if you were to visit the school now, more than twenty years later, and ask who was Li Zhongmei, the students would be able to tell you her story—her exclusion from the fundamentals of ballet, the string around her wrist, her discovery by Jia Zuoguang, even Comrade Tsang's defenestration of the kitten she tried to save.

This does not mean, after her triumphant performance in the final that first year, that everything became easy for Zhongmei, her life a dream like that of a flying apsara. For seven more years she endured the rigors of the Beijing Dance Academy, the torturous weight-loss costume, the high-stepping morning drill through the park, the calisthenics, the discipline, the constant demand to do better when she was doing the best she could. For seven more years, twice every year, she suffered that terrible journey from Beijing to Baoquanling and back, three days and two nights on trains in hard-seat class, with the long layover in Harbin, then those rattling, crowded buses to Hegang and Baoquanling. She wanted to see her family, but she dreaded that trip so much that her stomach tightened for days in advance and she lost her normally vigorous appetite.

Even Teacher Zhu, despite Zhongmei's demonstration of refinement, kept trying to find ways to keep her from taking the second year of fundamentals of ballet.

"Oh, you don't look good," she would frequently say as Zhongmei walked into the studio. "Why don't you go down to see the nurse, rest a bit. I think you're coming down with something."

"But I feel fine," Zhongmei would reply, wondering why this person continued to persecute her.

"Go down to the nurse," Teacher Zhu would order.

"You again!" the nurse would declare. "There's nothing wrong with you." Finally she sent Zhongmei back to Teacher Zhu with a note: "Zhongmei is perfectly healthy. Please do not send her to me again."

And then there was the time when she was a fourteen-year-old fourth-year student and her partner didn't catch her correctly as she landed after a difficult leap. She fell on the side of her ankle, heard a cracking sound, and then passed out from the pain. For the second time in her life she woke up in a hospital, and the doctor told her she had broken several bones in her foot.

"You'll be able to walk," the doctor said, "but probably with a limp."

"Will I be able to dance?" Zhongmei asked, not quite realizing the gravity of her situation.

"Dance?" the doctor said. He hesitated. He was a kind man. "We'll have to see."

Zhongmei gritted her teeth through the pain of six months of physical therapy before she was able to go into a dance studio again, but she did heal, she did dance again, and she graduated on time. The girl who defeated Teacher Zhu wasn't going to let broken bones stop her.

When it came time to graduate in 1984, Zhongmei was

widely deemed to be the best dancer in her class. A competition was held in one of Beijing's biggest theaters, with China's Minister of Culture in attendance. All the girls took part. Zhongmei won it. In fact, she won every major dance competition she entered for the next four years in a row.

But none of this success ever went to her head. Zhongmei remained modest and unassuming. She never forgot who she was or where she came from. She was always ready to help younger dance students, and whenever she happened to meet one from the countryside, especially one who doubted her ability to succeed in the midst of all the sophisticated big-city girls at the school, Zhongmei would tell her that nothing is impossible, if only you work hard and you believe in yourself.

At her graduation ceremony at the Beijing Dance Academy, Zhongmei was asked to make a speech. This is what she said:

> "I couldn't sleep last night because I knew that I'd be making a speech at graduation today, and I really didn't know what to say. I'm still not sure what to say, but I know I can't just make a few noises about how happy I am and how wonderful my experience has always been at the Beijing Dance Academy.
>
> "Of course, I am happy, I'm happy to graduate, very happy to have been named one of the top students. I appreciate the help and support I've gotten from my teachers and my

fellow students. You made it possible for me to have this great honor, and I'm very grateful and very moved."

Zhongmei stopped for a moment, fighting with her emotion.

"But I can't say that being here was always a happy experience. There were times, especially at the beginning, when I was miserable. I felt weak. I felt like I would never be able to succeed. I was told too often that because I'm from a rural area of China, a backward area compared to big cities like Beijing and Shanghai, that I would never be a good dancer. In China, as everybody knows, we have an expression—You have to throw away the broken pot. Well, I was the broken pot, and I was almost thrown away. I came close to being destroyed here, destroyed in spirit. Many times I wanted to give up. I almost did give up. I lost all confidence in myself and came to believe that, yes, I needed to be thrown away like a broken pot, that I could never be fixed. I cried often. And when I cried, I wondered: Why, if I'm a broken pot, did they take me here in the first place?

"Now I have the honor of graduating at the top of my class. I think that gives me the right to ask everybody to think about something. What if we have another girl from the countryside someday, and she doesn't look quite right? She has that blotched, sunburned skin of a country girl? She's treated as if she's deficient, backward, like a broken pot? What if this girl works hard? What if she gives her whole life to practicing, to trying to make herself better? And then what if she's told she's from the countryside and that's why she has to be thrown away? This little person, this eleven-year-old person, can be destroyed because of prejudice like that.

"I ask you to think about that. Anybody who is taken here, no matter where they come from, shouldn't they be given a fair chance?

"Luckily I have a strong will and in the end I didn't give up. I didn't give up because I didn't want to disappoint my parents or the people in my hometown who were so excited when I passed the auditions. Luckily for me, I had a good friend here who helped me get through the worst times. Luckily too, Vice Director Jia and my teachers paid attention to me before it was too late. I understand I was accepted at this school as a sort of experiment, to see what a coarse and unrefined farm girl could do. Well, maybe it's OK to use somebody for an experiment like that, but if you do, you have to realize that she also has a heart, that she's not a pot that can be ignored and then thrown away."

Zhongmei looked at her audience. All eyes were on her, Vice Director Jia's, Comrade Tsang's, Teacher Zhu's, and Teacher Peng's, and those of all the girls who had come to the Dance Academy when they were eleven years old. Xiaolan was there, and Zhongmei looked straight into her eyes and smiled.

"So, that's it," Zhongmei said. "My speech is finished. In the end, it all worked out. I am happy. Thank you for the opportunity to speak to you from my heart."

Zhongmei sat down. Her teachers and her fellow students applauded warmly. The ceremony continued with the granting of diplomas. When Zhongmei's turn came, she got her diploma and a red badge naming her the top graduate of the Beijing Dance Academy, class of 1984.

When she got to her seat, she looked at it, just a piece of baked clay with some Chinese characters stamped on it. And yet it meant everything to her. It meant that in the end it had all been worth it—the hunger strike, those terrible train rides, the four-o'clock mornings in studio two, the days spent on the floor in fundamentals of ballet, all those Sundays when she didn't go with the other girls for ice sticks in Tiananmen Square. Zhongmei clutched her red badge and fought back tears. It meant that she had nothing to regret, that if she could turn back the clock to that day in Baoquanling when her sister first mentioned the auditions in Beijing, she would grit her teeth, summon up her courage, and dare to do it all over again.

李忠梅

Acknowledgments

I want to thank my sister, Judy Peritz, for suggesting the idea for this book—as well as for being a great sister over the years. Sincere thanks too to the editors at Alfred A. Knopf Books for Young Readers, especially Nancy Hinkel, whose numerous suggestions, ideas, and devoted attention went way beyond the call of duty. I am listed as the author of this book, but Nancy played such a big role in it that I feel it's unfair her name isn't also on the title page. Jon Segal, my brilliant as usual editor at Knopf, introduced me to Nancy, and I thank him for that. My agent, Kathy Robbins, was by my side as always with her indispensable counsel, both practical and creative. And, of course, there's Zhongmei herself, the Faithful Plum of the title whose story I tell and who, along with our son, Elias, to whom this book is dedicated, is at the center not just of this true tale of adversity and triumph, but of my life. To her I owe more than mere words can express.

李忠梅

About the Author

*G*rowing up in the small town of East Haddam, Connecticut, Richard Bernstein always dreamed of seeing the world, and after he finished university, he figured a great way to do that would be to become a newspaper reporter. So he became a foreign correspondent for *Time* magazine and then the *New York Times*, which sent him (all expenses paid!) to lots of countries, including Hong Kong, China, Thailand, Indonesia, Vietnam, France, Germany, Poland, South Africa, Mozambique, and about twenty others. Along the way, he wrote thousands of newspaper articles and seven books, mostly for grown-ups. *Faithful Plum* is his first book for young readers, but he's sure it won't be his last. After moving around for most of his life, Richard settled in Brooklyn, New York, where he lives with his wife, Zhongmei (who *is* Faithful Plum!), their son, Elias, and their cat, Lucky.